The Caning of Charles Sum

WITNESS TO HISTORY

Peter Charles Hoffer and Williamjames Hull Hoffer, *Series Editors*

THE CANING OF CHARLES SUMNER

HONOR, IDEALISM, AND THE ORIGINS OF THE CIVIL WAR

WILLIAMJAMES HULL HOFFER

The Johns Hopkins University Press | Baltimore

© 2010 The Johns Hopkins University Press
All rights reserved. Published 2010
Printed in the United States of America on acid-free paper

9 8 7 6 5 4 3 2 1

The Johns Hopkins University Press
2715 North Charles Street
Baltimore, Maryland 21218-4363
www.press.jhu.edu

Library of Congress Cataloging-in-Publication Data
Hoffer, Williamjames.
The caning of Charles Sumner : honor, idealism, and the origins of the Civil
War / Williamjames Hull Hoffer.
    p.   cm. — (Witness to history)
Includes bibliographical references and index.
ISBN-13: 978-0-8018-9468-8 (hardcover : alk. paper)
ISBN-10: 0-8018-9468-9 (hardcover : alk. paper)
ISBN-13: 978-0-8018-9469-5 (pbk. : alk. paper)
ISBN-10: 0-8018-9469-7 (pbk. : alk. paper)
    1. Sumner, Charles, 1811–1874. 2. Brooks, Preston S. (Preston Smith),
1819–1857. 3. Assault and battery—United States—History—19th century.
4. Legislators—United States—Biography. 5. Idealism, American—Political
aspects—History—19th century. 6. Honor—Political aspects—United
States—History—19th century. 7. United States—History—Civil War,
1861–1865—Causes. 8. Slavery—Political aspects—United States—History—
19th century. 9. United States—Politics and government—1849–1861. I. Title.
    E434.8.H64 2010
    973.7′11—dc22   2009035569

A catalog record for this book is available from the British Library.

Special discounts are available for bulk purchases of this book. For
more information, please contact Special Sales at 410-516-6936 or
specialsales@press.jhu.edu.

The Johns Hopkins University Press uses environmentally friendly book
materials, including recycled text paper that is composed of at least
30 percent post-consumer waste, whenever possible. All of our book papers
are acid-free, and our jackets and covers are printed on paper with
recycled content.

CONTENTS

The Caning of Charles Sumner

INTRODUCTION

ON MAY 22, 1856, Democratic Congressman Preston S. Brooks of South Carolina repeatedly struck Republican Senator Charles Sumner of Massachusetts over the head with a cane, leaving the senator bloody and unconscious on the floor of the United States Senate. Within hours it was national news. Within days it had become the first national media circus. In the election that November, Sumner's Republican Party, formed a little over two years before, came within two states of gaining the White House. Four years later, it would succeed. Illinois assemblyman Abraham Lincoln led a Republican victory sweep of northern electoral votes. Within a month of his inauguration, the nation entered the Civil War. The war led to the loss of over six hundred thousand lives, the Confederacy was devastated, and four million slaves were freed. The United States would never be the same.

The caning of Charles Sumner, or the Brooks-Sumner affair as it was then known, did not cause the Civil War. The rifts that led to the war gave rise to hundreds of such contests before the bloodletting began in earnest. But in the caning one can see, as if in a perfect mirror, the sectional differences, differences over the idealism of abolitionism and the honor of the slaveholders, that split the nation and brought the war. For these two men, in many important ways, personified the clash between North and South. Their politics, their culture, their society, and the place where they came to blows—Washington, D.C.—reflected that sectionalism. It resonated in every debate on Capitol Hill, shaped party politics, dictated the outcome of elections, and made compromise impossible and animosity implacable. In sum, the caning was more than a clash between two men. It was a microcosm of the crisis of antebellum American politics, a witness to the contrast of the two states, South Carolina and Massachusetts, that produced a Brooks and a Sumner.

What seems at first a simple confrontation of opposites, however, was in fact a far more complex series of events, riven with contingencies and ironic outcomes. These two men were both lawyers who believed in the rule of law and celebrated the Constitution, and yet both saw exceptions to settled law in the ideal of human equality and in the acts that honor dictated. For abolitionist consciences and honor-bound consciences answered not to settled statutes or common-law precepts of courts but to higher laws that excused certain kinds of lawlessness.

That these two sets of precepts clashed on the floor of the Senate was itself an irony, for in the hallowed Old Senate Chamber the great lawgivers of the previous generation—Henry Clay, John C. Calhoun, and Daniel Webster—had found in acts of Congress a way to avoid national division. The caning of Sumner by Brooks signaled how frail congressional accommodation, compromise, and civility had become in the second half of the 1850s.

Although both men were elected members of Congress, when they joined in its debates they spoke for their own culture, society, and party. Ambitious men—capable of unscrupulous acts and biting oratory—they did not see any need to curb themselves. Historians have condemned their generation as blunderers, but a longer view sees Sumner and Brooks as representative, for as one member of the generation would later tell a political gathering, the conflict between slavery and freedom was fast becoming "irrepressible."

The goal here is to take an event and make it come alive, returning the reader to a time and place, in order to see it as it looked to those alive then, but with the advantage of historical insight. The caning of Charles Sumner easily lends itself to this purpose. A dramatic event taking place in a short compass of time, highly visible and much commented on, it changed the course of history. After, if not before, the caning, Brooks and Sumner became larger-than-life figures. Their combat, although one-sided at the time, would within days encompass the entire range of gallantry, knavery, courage, cowardice, calculation, and temper of the age.

The story has captivated historians. Some view Sumner as a self-seeking demagogue, pitching the nation into a frenzy of animosity with his indelicate fulminations. He brought the war closer in their view. Others regard Sumner as an avatar of radical reform, dedicated to human equality and determined to raise the lowest man—the slave—to the level of equal citizen. Some historians regard Brooks as a deeply troubled man, who gave way to a frenzy of violence. Others see his acts and words well within a carefully delineated code of shame and honor, in which no one could ignore the incitements of Sumner's reckless rhetoric. Indeed, so sharply etched are the differences in the interpretations of the two men, and consequently of the event itself, that a balanced account seemed almost beyond our abilities.

One can, of course, simply recover and repeat the primary sources. These include the letters that Brooks wrote to his family, an unpublished defense of his actions (probably the legal brief he had prepared for the trial), the testimony taken before the House and Senate select committees, and newspaper reports of the event, the trial, and the reactions of political leaders throughout the country. But upon closer examination, these primary sources are sharply divided, seeing and speaking according to sectional and party affiliation. Like the many witnesses in the classic movie *Rashomon*, no two observers saw the same thing. The barest facts are uncontroverted: two politicians come to blows; one is martyred or derided for faking; the other is celebrated for his daring or berated for his brute cruelty. The receptions are the opposite in each section of the country.

Sumner had provoked Brooks by ridiculing Brooks's cousin, Senator Andrew P. Butler, the state of South Carolina, and the entire slaveholding South in his speech "The Crime against Kansas." After a short trial for a simple assault, Brooks received a fine of three hundred dollars. He resigned from the House, was reelected by his district, and died a year later of a throat infection. Sumner did not return to his duties in the Senate full time until 1860, after which he had a distinguished career in that body until his death in 1874.

Behind every simple fact, however, there are unanswered questions. Brooks was applauded in the South for his actions because he defended the "honor" of South Carolina and the standing and pride of his distinguished family. But the very notion of honor was a complicated one. For some it was an unspoken but all-pervasive code of good conduct. One must never be shamed or act in a shameful manner at the risk of public opprobrium, and one must never allow another to bring disgrace on one's name or that of family members. Only certain members of society had honor, however. Only whites had a degree of pride or honor that had to be upheld, but each person had to defer to the status of those higher in the social order. Slaves had no respectable rank, no honor, and could not claim the rites or rights that the honor system conferred. A man with no honor was not entitled to be treated honorably. Although some historians contrast the honor system with a system of guilt, the two notions coexisted and were mutually supporting. Nor did religion, with its notions of charity to one's condemners and turning the other cheek to insult, find fault with honor-bound conscience. Although some ministers in the South did denounce dueling, for instance, and there are sermons against being overbearing and prideful, they understood and accepted the dictates of honor.

Sumner had abused Butler and other Democratic defenders of slavery's expansion in vicious language that both sides had polished for thirty years. Sumner's incivility had a myriad of precedent. But Brooks and Sumner were equals in rank and status. Indeed, Sumner was the older man with the higher office. Brooks should have challenged him as he did others before and after the incident. Why did he choose to cane Sumner instead? Why did Sumner not defend himself? Why did the witnesses, themselves members of Congress and the sergeant at arms, not intervene?

The legal proceedings themselves are also a curiosity. Surely the cane attack was an aggravated assault. Why was Brooks not charged with a more serious offense than simple assault? Why was the sentence so light? Why did the House not expel him, nor the Senate censure him? The investigation into these vexing questions becomes more complicated the further we probe the events following them. A centerpiece of political journalism through the election, the caning was hardly mentioned after 1856. What had occurred to push it off the pages? Was it swallowed up in the Kansas statehood controversy? Did the Republicans decide that it was more of an embarrassment than a banner issue? Lincoln never mentioned it. What is the significance of any one clash in such a maelstrom of discontent, argument, and political maneuvering as the politics of 1857–61?

But if the rush to war gained new momentum from the caning, then should we brush it aside so easily? If the war was inevitable, no single event was essential in explanation of the causes of the war. Were the two populations represented in this clash so different that their conflict was bound to happen? Perhaps—but again the caning gives us a chance to examine that question. For Sumner and Brooks were representative of those very same great forces. Or perhaps the caning was the proverbial black swan.

The black swan is an unexpected detail that challenges a basic understanding, which in turn was based on an immense amount of observational evidence. We assume that swans are always white because all the swans we have seen are white. Seeing one black swan destroys that assumption and calls all of that knowledge into doubt. It would be a mistake to assume thereafter that we will now see black swans frequently. While the one black swan disproved the notion about the whiteness of all swans, it should not lead to the unsupported notion that black swans are more frequent than they actually are.[1] The same set of reasoning applies to the caning of Charles Sumner. Without further investigation, we should not assume that caning was a way of life or more prevalent that it actually was.

Surely, some readers will find that the incident stirs deep feelings in themselves. One of the purposes of this type of book is to enable readers, particularly students, to recapture some of the drama of the past while standing far enough removed from it to examine why they respond to those events as they do. Many of us will sympathize with one or the other party because of our political beliefs, the nature of the clash, or where we were reared. We may take for granted what Sumner espoused—the equality of Americans regardless of race, opposition to slavery, and the strong moral component of our laws and institutions—and be shocked that these founding principles were once matters of violent contention. We may feel strongly that it was wrong for Brooks to assault someone while he was seated and unarmed, and even more so to assault him so violently. Then again, we may come to feel that Brooks had reason to be furious with Sumner, for Sumner appeared to Brooks to heap scorn on hearth and home, family, and all that was good in the southern heritage. The reader may sympathize with a man who sought to defend his kin against cruel, abusive language. Who would not strike out in whatever way they could when confronted with such insults?

Our feelings about the incident may also be colored by our anticipation of the war that followed. We may well be tempted to look on this clash as a tale of two men behaving like ill-tempered children, and as a result we careened into an avoidable, bloody war of terrible carnage. If we have a conspiratorial or suspicious bent, we may wonder about the motivations of two powerful men seeking to determine the destinies of millions without sufficient thought about the consequences.

Facing such strong and suddenly aroused feeling, we must remind ourselves to be historically minded, to see the world as they saw it in their time and place. When we have done that, we gain a favorable vantage point to see what was obscure and perceive the liveliness of the scene inside a larger view. It is this simultaneous immediacy and distance in the study of history that makes it such an important part of critical thinking. We come to see the casual racism of the day in dual perspective, then and now, empathetically and critically. For we have enough in common with the Americans of the mid-nineteenth century for us to relate to their concerns with an open mind. The language of their politics is similar to ours if not the same. The values of words such as liberty, democracy, justice, and equality are the same in impact if not in exact meaning. The three branches of government are still there, and visits to the Old Senate Chamber are possible by arrangement with the Capitol Police and the National Park Service. In a nation that has reenactments of Civil War battles accurate to the last coat button and victual, we are not that far away from the world of Charles Sumner and Preston S. Brooks.

With these issues in mind, the following pages tackle the story of the caning of Charles Sumner. Chapter 1, "One Minute," relates the incident in detail by weaving together the different strands of the story from a variety of sources. It proceeds to introduce our main protagonists as products of their home states and tracks the key events in which those states played their part. The contrasts and the similarities between them become apparent. Chapter 2, "A Machine That Would Go of Itself?," traces the development of the debate over the expansion of slavery from its origins in the constitutional founding era to Sumner's "Crime against Kansas" oration. It is a complex tangle of political rivalries and legal developments. Only within that context can we begin to comprehend the language of Sumner's speech, its genesis, and the part the caning is to play in future events.

Chapter 3, "Immediate Aftermath," lays out the immediate investigation, criminal proceedings, media circus, and general commotion that followed the caning. In that series of events, we can find the overlapping and interacting realms of politics, law, and public conversation, which in turn lay bare the competing notions of freedom, nationhood, and manhood within the larger polity. Chapter 4, "A Long, Winding Road," traces our story out to the start of the Civil War. Only by analyzing those subsequent events can we truly place the caning within the larger story of a nation traveling along a path toward war, destruction, and reconstitution. Chapter 5, "Honor, Idealism, and Inevitability," assays the ways in which the caning changed American history. The book concludes with an epilogue, which gives a brief application of the lessons of the caning to more recent events.

1 | ONE MINUTE

IT WAS the 22nd of May in the year 1856. Outside the U.S. Capitol, Congressman Preston Smith Brooks, Democrat from South Carolina, waited for his quarry to emerge. His target, Senator Charles Sumner, Republican from Massachusetts, had recently made a speech entitled "The Crime against Kansas" in which he had heaped insults onto the South, its representatives, and the state of South Carolina and one of its senators, Andrew Pickens Butler, a cousin of Brooks's father, among others.

Brooks cut a less-than-elegant figure pacing in front of the still-under-construction Capitol. With his long, severe face, topped by a shock of wavy black hair, his chin elongated further by a goatee, he resembled more a city profligate than a country gentleman. His glossy waistcoat and tie were elegant, but he was weary. He had spent the previous night with his close friend and ally, South Carolina Congressman Laurence M. Keitt, planning, drinking, and ranting about what he would do when the time came. His limp—the result of a hip injury suffered in a duel—grew more noticeable. He had with him a cane, but he gripped it not to support himself so much as to test its properties as a cudgel. Eventually, he grew frustrated and decided to seek out Sumner in the Senate chamber.

Once there, he spied Sumner still at his desk on the Senate floor. The chamber had largely emptied, the spittoons still full and the air still smoky. In one of those twists of fate, Sumner was applying his stamp to copies of the speech so he could mail them to his admirers at taxpayer expense. Designed to resemble the amphitheaters of classical Greece, the chamber was a large semicircle seventy-five feet long and fifty feet wide. The ceiling was a half dome, and the front of the room had a wide arch with marble columns. In front of these columns were the dais for the president of the Senate and the desks of other Senate officials. Two visitors' galleries supported by iron columns encircled the sides and back. Paintings, including Rembrandt Peale's portrait of George Washington, hung on the walls. On the floor of the chamber, arranged in a semicircle facing the dais, were the mahogany desks of the senators, which were the only offices they possessed at this time. It would soon be given over to the U.S. Supreme Court (moving out of its drafty and mildewed basement quarters), but in its time, the Old Senate Chamber had witnessed the greatest oratory in the new nation's history. Here, in 1850, Henry Clay and Daniel Webster had pleaded for the Union, and John C. Calhoun warned of a dire fate if the California Compromise bills did not pass.

Brooks sat in the back row of the chamber and waited. His friend, Virginia Representative Henry A. Edmundson, asked if he was now a senator. Senators were elected by their states' legislatures. Brooks replied fiercely that he wanted to upbraid Sumner but could not while ladies were present. He motioned to one particular woman who was sitting not far from Sumner at the side of the chamber. Impatient with her persistence in his place of business, Brooks asked the sergeant at arms to remove her as this was no place for ladies. But, as the Senate had adjourned for the day, nothing could be done but wait. For what must have seemed an eternity, Brooks did just that until she left the room. Accompanied by Keitt, Brooks approached the still-seated Sumner.

From the rear, Sumner seemed impressive. Brooks could not see the heavy but handsome features, but the mane of dark hair flowing down a massive neck to powerful hunched shoulders gave the impression of great strength. Compared to Brooks, Sumner dressed simply. He was not a wealthy man, but he preferred the mien of a man of the people in any case. Absorbed in his business, he did not appear to hear Brooks's arrival.

Brooks later alleged that he uttered the following words: "Mr. Sumner, I have read your speech with care and as much impartiality as was possible and I feel it my duty to tell you that you have libeled my State and slandered a relative who is aged and absent and I am come to punish you for it."[1] Brooks implied that he had come around the desk to face Sumner. It was a long speech, and had Brooks delivered it as he said, surely Sumner would have risen from his desk to reply. In fact, before he completed whatever he said to Sumner, Brooks lifted his cane, specially selected for this sanguinary purpose, and began to hit Sumner on the head with as much force as Brooks could muster. The initial blow stunned Sumner and drove him back against his chair. Disoriented, he could not rise because the chair was mounted to the floor.

Brooks did not stop with a single blow. He continued to assail Sumner with increasing fury until the cane shattered, and even then he did not slacken his assault. Sumner thrashed about, attempting to ward off the blows, but pinned beneath his desk, he was trapped. He did not remember that the chair was on a set of tracks and could not be dislodged except by pushing straight back. Bloodied, confused, and desperate to end the attack, Sumner managed at last to dislodge the desk from its bolted moorings. Staggering away from Brooks, he stumbled into the aisle. Brooks pursued him. As Sumner collapsed to the ground unconscious from the blows to his head, Congressman Edwin B. Morgan of New York caught him, the two men striking the ground in a heap.

By this time all those present in the chamber had heard the commotion. Their responses were not those of shocked passersby, nor those of caregivers. Instead, so divided was the Congress by sectional and partisan feeling that they acted the role of sectional and party men. John J. Crittenden, a long-serving Democratic senator from the border state of Kentucky, came down the aisle and implored Brooks not to kill Sumner. Keitt blocked Crittenden's way, with his own cane raised high, making clear the price for interference. Robert Toombs, senator from Georgia, rose to the defense of Crittenden. He did not want an innocent to be injured. He later stated that he would not have tried to stop Brooks because "I . . . approved it [the caning]."[2] Note that Toombs did not see the caning as a crime, but as a political act. Toombs would be a major player when Georgia held its secession convention, and he would help the secessionists win the day.

Keitt was unable to stop Representative Ambrose S. Murray from restraining Brooks. Murray would later testify that he had no great concern for Sumner's well-being but feared that Brooks had lost control and might have killed Sumner if not blocked from further mayhem. With the aid of a page and the sergeant at arms, Morgan, like Murray a representative from New York, helped the now-conscious Sumner stumble to a cloakroom. He made a ghastly sight. The wounds and gashes on his head had bled profusely. His shirt and coat were drenched with blood. Sweaty and disheveled, he cut a pathetic figure. They gave him some water and someone fetched a doctor. After the doctor, Cornelius Boyle, had closed the two gashes on his head with rough stitches, Sumner's friend and fellow Massachusetts Senator Henry

"The Assault in the U.S. Senate Chamber on Senator Sumner." Unknown Artist and Engraver, Woodcut. Cover, *Frank Leslie's Illustrated Newspaper*, June 7, 1856, with a depiction of the assault in the lower left corner.

Wilson, who had rushed back into the chamber upon hearing of the assault, helped him to a carriage. They went to Sumner's lodgings.

Brooks too received medical help. One of his backswings was so vigorous that it cut him above the eye, which required some attention before he strode out of the chamber. He made sure he kept the head of the cane with him as it was gold and of some value. Accompanied by Keitt and Edmundson, he returned to his rooms he had rented for his stay in Washington. Shortly thereafter he reported to the authorities what he had done. A warrior tradition requires that the taker of fair vengeance must report his deeds. He was not afraid to face the law having accomplished his objective. He had given the loathsome Yankee a "redress of a personal wrong."[3]

The assault itself lasted about a minute. One lawmaker battered another into insensibility on the floor of one of the most revered, historic arenas for public business in full view of several other lawmakers and onlookers, many of whom had no objection to a man beating another unarmed man senseless. What could possibly explain such a bizarre spectacle?

Melees in Congress

It was not that violence was unknown to the Congress. In fact, the two houses of government were widely known for some of the more ridiculous altercations in the country's history. It befitted the new nation's rustic character to have its legislators not only spit their tobacco juice on the floor but occasionally fight with more than words if the impulse took them. One could tell a history of the country from its congressional brawls. One scholar has argued that a culture of honor framed the new country's political culture. It may be hard to see the ideal of honor in such contretemps, but it is there.

The most famous and earliest brawl took place between Matthew Lyon from Vermont and Roger Griswold from Connecticut. Lyon was a Republican, not the modern-day institution, but a party formed by Thomas Jefferson and other like-minded men. They had rebelled against the nationalist, commerce-oriented, and friendly-to-Britain Federalists like Griswold. The country was fiercely divided about whether to support revolutionary France or parliamentary Britain. The Federalists held the presidency under unpopular John Adams and delicate majorities in both houses. The Republicans were full of the nervousness that accompanies a lack of power and a political philosophy that distrusted government.

The confrontation stemmed from a shouting match on January 30, 1798, which had begun with Lyon's loud remarks about the perfidies of Connecticut Federalists, continued with Griswold's retort about Lyon's early departure from the Continental Army, and culminated in Lyon spitting his tobacco juice into Griswold's face. Whether Griswold's sole response at that time—to remove his handkerchief and wipe the expectoration from his face—was the result of a gentleman's restraint or the intervention of his cooler-headed friends we do not know. However, when the House declined to expel Lyon for this offense—the Federalists did not have the necessary two-thirds—Griswold took the punishment into his own hands. On February 15, he waited until after the Morning Prayer to approach Lyon while the latter was seated at his desk. Exactly as Brooks would do some fifty-eight years later, Griswold began striking him with his cane about the head and shoulders.

Unlike Sumner, Lyon was not pinioned beneath his desk and fought back. He managed to secure a pair of tongs from a nearby fireplace and returned blows. As the Speaker of the House called for some of the crowded House to break the two up, they grappled with one another, reportedly to the cheers of their various supporters as if they were gladiators in the arena. Eventually, some did hear the Speaker's call. The two men were separated, only to reengage moments later when Griswold came back to finish the matter. Both escaped punishment. Many were ashamed of the disrepute heaped on the chamber that such raucous behavior generated, but others were amused, including possibly the newspaper caricaturist who publicized the squabble, making both representatives look buffoonish.

These were not the statesmen who called for independence, but the younger generation who had helped win it. Lyon came as an indentured servant from Ireland and fought with Ethan Allen at Fort Ticonderoga. Griswold belonged to a prosperous, old New England family. Both felt strongly about the merits of their respective positions and the evils of their opponents. Their dispute illustrated the best and worst of the political system. The fighting would erupt on a small scale with the occasional fracas, but the nation would be relatively free from massive uprisings.

The next notable confrontation involved one of the founders of Texas, Sam Houston. In 1832 the House reprimanded him for caning Representative William Stanbery, former Democrat and then a Whig from Ohio, on Pennsylvania Avenue. Stanbery had accused Houston of profiting from government liquor contracts linked to President Andrew Jackson's Indian Removal Act of 1830. Perhaps the lenience of the punishment came from Stanbery's spirited defense: his pistol misfired in the altercation, sparing the life of the future victor of the Battle of San Jacinto. Houston's attorney in the criminal trial, national anthem lyrics writer Francis Scott Key, managed to secure a mere fine and warning for the attack that sent Stanbery to the hospital. Jackson happily remitted the fine at Houston's request. Old Hickory more than sympathized, for he had been an avid duelist and well understood the need to cane the rascal Stanbery.

Maine Representative Jonathan Cilley was not so lucky. In 1838, he died in a duel with William J. Graves, a Whig from Kentucky and protégé of Henry

Clay. Oddly enough, the duelists felt it necessary to go to four rounds of rifle shots over a challenge Cilley had refused to accept from a third party who had delivered it through Graves. Graves took it upon himself to issue his own challenge.

Many clashes involved Southerners finding fault with other Southerners. William B. Campbell, future governor of Tennessee, scuffled with fellow Tennessean Abram P. Maury, a West Point graduate, behind the Speaker's chair. This 1838 incident ended with Campbell holding Maury by the hair while pummeling him in the face. The year 1840 saw two clashes with canes. In one North Carolina's Jesse Bynum went after Rice Garland from Louisiana. Kenneth Rayner and William Montgomery, also North Carolinians, broke each other's canes over their respective heads.

In the contentious 1850s political brawls grew in number. One cannot say that the rate of extralegal affrays increased, but they exhibited an ideological focus instead of mere personal pique. Taking exception to *New York Tribune* editor and abolitionist Horace Greeley's ridiculing of him during the Speaker election controversy of January 1856, Arkansas Representative Albert Rust struck Greeley twice in one day, once just outside the Capitol and again later in front of Greeley's hotel. Unlike Sumner's extended ailment, Greeley took the incidents in stride and returned to New York to continue the fight against slavery. In 1858 during another debate on admitting Kansas, a bench-clearing brawl broke out on the floor of the House chamber. It only dissipated when Wisconsin's John F. "Bowie Knife" Potter grabbed the hair of Mississippi's William Barksdale and a toupee came off in full view of the assembly. Potter exclaimed, "I've scalped him!" Amid peals of laughter the House returned to order.[4]

All for Honor

The weapon of choice for congressional battery was the cane. During that period of time from the eighteenth to the nineteenth century, certain paraphernalia established one's status as a gentleman, and that status mattered. Canes were a highly valued personal item, part of male dress. Lower-class men did not use canes, nor did women. Thus, the cane marked a man so that others might see him. The cane, in other words, was part of a system of visible signs and signals. That system did not so much depict rank and hierarchy, for the cane remained a necessary accessory to middle-class men, as the marker of another, far less visible set of signs and symbols. A cane was a sign that its bearer understood and accepted a canon, or set of conventions, about proper behavior. A concern with proper behavior governed much of their conduct, although there was a widening gulf between northern and southern conceptions over appropriate models.

We know it today as the honor culture. In its most exaggerated form, men would fire pistols at one another over a perceived slight to one's respectability, one's family, or one's region. Just such a conflict ended the life of Alexander Hamilton, a founding father, first secretary of the treasury, coauthor of *The Federalist Papers*, and one of the most important political figures of the early national period. His killer was none other than Aaron Burr, Jefferson's current vice president and one of the forgotten founders of American democracy. Their dispute began, as it commonly did, with a publication of supposed misdeeds and one "despicable" act.[5] Burr blamed Hamilton for the accusations and their possible effect on his failed New York gubernatorial campaign. In an exchange of letters, Burr and Hamilton careened toward what one may loosely describe as "an affair of honor." An examination of it reveals something of the honor culture.

On July 11, 1804, they met at a prearranged location, a sandbar off Weehawken, New Jersey, across the Hudson River from their homes in New York City. Although what transpired next is in dispute, the result is not. A pistol shot from Burr lodged in Hamilton's spine, causing his agonizing death one day later. Burr was unharmed, at least physically. Hamilton's supporters, however, made the duel out to be a slaughter. Hamilton had confided to a friend before the duel that he planned to "waste" his shot—firing in the air so as not to harm his opponent. Burr had to flee the area as both New York and New Jersey authorities sought him for violating their laws against dueling. Although this duel was extraordinary in its casting, outcome, and notoriety, in its specifics it was an ordinary encounter pursued according to an agreed-upon set of rules.

Later codified after a fashion in an Irish document, subsequently in a South Carolina version, the Code Duello demanded strict adherence if it were to perform its function of resolving disputes. It was not a bloodthirsty document, preferring instead to offer several ways for honor to be satisfied rather than the proverbial pistols at dawn. It was, however, much more elaborate than the duel at high noon we know from Westerns. Each party had seconds who were to perform the intermediary functions necessary to the procedure for challenging, offering solutions, and, if necessary, making the final arrangements for the encounter. As the author of the definitive version for South Carolina wrote, "I believe that nine duels out of ten, if not ninety-nine out of a hundred, originate in the want of experience in the seconds."[6] At all times, parties were to respect one another and presume a form of equality. It is not hard to see in these exchanges of notes, charges, countercharges, and negotiations a legalistic society in microcosm. Perfectly suited for the notoriously litigious American market, it is a wonder it took until the 1830s to reach the United States in published form.

Why, then, did Preston Brooks not issue a challenge under the rules of the Code Duello? According to his testimony at his subsequent trial and a congressional investigation, he did not believe a man like Charles Sumner would accept one. With regard to this alleged supposition, it is quite likely Sumner would have refused. Dueling had long been outlawed in Washington, D.C., as it had almost everywhere. Northerners were quite open about their contempt for what many considered a barbaric practice.

Was Brooks being honest about this explanation? He had thought a great deal about the encounter. He also testified to wanting to treat Sumner appropriately. Thrashing someone was reserved for an inferior. One whipped a slave for disobedience and hit a slave for disrespectful speech. Punishing someone like a child across the knee was commonly practiced, and thrashing someone with a cane was fairly close. However, Sumner's surprise and Brooks's adoption of this method of redress also denoted a vast gulf between the Massachusetts senator and the representative from the Edgefield district of South Carolina.

A Tale of Two States, Two Sections, Two Men

For Sumner and Brooks, more so even than Hamilton and Burr, state loyalties stood for something. In 1856, leading figures in public life still identified themselves as Massachusetts men or South Carolina men rather than Americans. Their loyalty to their states was more than mere political attachment. They believed that they owed their states a special affection. That kind of loyalty would display itself when men as honorable as Robert E. Lee would abjure their oaths of allegiance and their duty to their country to follow their state into secession. What was more, the lines of attachment and influence ran in both directions. For the experience, values, customs, and indeed the history of their respective states ran through Sumner's and Brooks's family histories. Thus, in some sense their conflict was the confluence of the completely different historical paths of Massachusetts and South Carolina.

It is commonplace to assert that a leading cause of the Civil War, and the crisis years of the 1850s that preceded it, was sectionalism. North versus South, Yankee versus Planter, free labor versus slavery, and, to a lesser extent, industrial and commercial versus agricultural and rural are some of the many versions of this sectional divide. Some have gone so far as to describe the two regions as two different nations with different cultures, ideologies, and societies, an argument that gained more and more weight at the time as conflict followed conflict. But what were the actual differences between these two sides?

In many respects Charles Sumner and Preston Smith Brooks were alike. They were both well educated at the foremost school in their respective states, Harvard and the future University of South Carolina. They came from distinguished if not elite families. Although Sumner was eight years older, their generations were not entirely different. They came from old stock families that could trace their roots to the founding of their respective colonies. Finally, they were both admitted to the bar and practiced law for a time before settling into their careers in politics. However, there were important differences, which stemmed from the distinct histories of their home states.

Sumner, the older of the two, came from the older settlement. From the inception of the Massachusetts Bay Colony in the 1630s, its history was as different from that of South Carolina as one could imagine between two parts of the same nation. Charles I was largely tricked into giving a charter to the Massachusetts Bay Company. The managers and a majority of the colonists were devoted members of the Church of England, known as Puritans for their almost fanatical belief in cleansing that church of its Roman Catholic elements. As John Winthrop, their astute leader and governor, declared, their purpose would be to establish a model community, "the city on a hill," which would serve as a beacon to England and the rest of the world as to the proper practice of religion in the New World. Although tested severely by starving times, Indian wars, sectarian combats, smallpox outbreaks, and even an earthquake, the first generations of New Englanders built towns, met in representative assemblies, and "hived out" over the landscape. Massachusetts would absorb Plymouth, send its sons and daughters to New Hampshire,

Connecticut, Rhode Island, and Maine, and become what one historian has called the nursery of the English Empire. By the end of the colonial period their overflow would reach into New York, the Ohio Valley, and even the Great Lakes region.

Life in Massachusetts was physically hard, but with the exception of a few personal servants and some laborers in the cities, the white population did not purchase many slaves. This was less due to moral scruple than to the short growing season in the Northeast. Nevertheless, one of the first great antislavery tracts in the Western world came from the pen of a Puritan magistrate, Samuel Sewall's *The Selling of Joseph* (1700). In it, Boston's Sewall decried, "How horrible is the Uncleanness, Mortality, if not Murder, that the Ships are guilty of that bring great Crouds of these miserable Men, and Women. Methinks, when we are bemoaning the barbarous Usage of our Friends and Kinsfolk in Africa: it might not be unseasonable to enquire whether we are not culpable in forcing the Africans to become Slaves amongst our selves."[7] Slavery would be legal in the Commonwealth until 1780, when justice William Cushing of the Supreme Judicial Court in *Commonwealth v. Jennison* told the jury, "But whatever sentiments have formerly prevailed in this particular or slid in upon us by the example of others, a different idea has taken place with the people of America, more favorable to the natural rights of mankind, and to that natural, innate desire of Liberty, with which Heaven (without regard to color, complexion, or shape of noses—features) has inspired all the human race. And upon this ground our Constitution of Government, by which the people of this Commonwealth have solemnly bound themselves, sets out with declaring that all men are born free and equal—and that every subject is entitled to liberty, and to have it guarded by the laws, as well as life and property—and in short is totally repugnant to the idea of being born slaves. This being the case, I think the idea of slavery is inconsistent with our own conduct and Constitution."[8]

Massachusetts regarded itself as the cockpit of the American Revolution. Its leaders—John Hancock, Samuel Adams, and John Adams, among others—had done much to bring about the separation of the thirteen colonies from the home country and contributed greatly to the successful conclusion of the Revolution. Although its influence, and that of its politicians, had declined along with its economic fortunes thereafter, it could claim to be the progenitor of two presidents, the father and son John and John Quincy Adams, as well as the nursery to others such as Vermont's Franklin Pierce, by the time of the caning. Massachusetts statesmen such as Daniel Webster had promoted the concept of rule of law. Massachusetts historians such as John Bancroft and Francis Parkman established the genre of American historical writing.

During Sumner's childhood, Massachusetts was successfully reinventing herself. Instead of the monopoly of Puritanism, there was religious toleration and a proliferation of denominations, including Roman Catholicism. The second great awakening of evangelical preaching roared through the state and would include in its converts Charles Sumner, among others, in the burgeoning abolitionist movement it helped inspire. Instead of subsistence farming, the backcountry remade itself into truck farms and cottage producers for the new mill towns. The state had maintained its sharpness in business, with a new emphasis on finance and industry. We should not confuse this market revolution development with the heavy industry of post–Civil War America, but its impact on Massachusetts was nonetheless profound. Massachusetts was at the forefront of a technological, transportation, communications, and commercial revolution.

The Bay State was one of the first to develop a canal system, then, more extensively, a railroad network. Telegraph lines crisscrossed the state, connecting her to national and world markets. Textile and other clothing industries made the state the destination for factory workers—first farm girls, then immigrants from overseas. The so-called Lowell System mills in northeastern Massachusetts were small operations by today's standards, but they constituted a critical break from past practice. Instead of an apprentice system for the making of shoes, tools, and other goods, or the piecework system of farming out textile manufacturing to local households, the Lowell System employed hundreds of workers in sizable buildings, or manufactories—factories—that were powered by nearby streams and rivers. The machinery the workers tended was a substantial investment in know-how and capital. Massachusetts had seen the future and it was in mass production.

Charles Sumner's Boston benefited in many ways from this accumulation of wealth. Sumner grew up in a state that cherished its Yankee traditions at the same time its economic transformation was tearing that traditional fabric to shreds. The Brahmins of Beacon Hill were an elite group under siege from not only the increasingly foreign-born immigrants of the 1840s and afterward but also a cultural flowering that broke over their conservative world in successive waves.

In addition to producing the novelists and short-story writers Nathaniel Hawthorne and Herman Melville, Massachusetts provided a home for the Transcendentalist movement of Ralph Waldo Emerson, Henry David Thoreau, and others; reform utopias such as Brook Farm; educational experiments such as Bronson Alcott's "Temple School"; and the publication of literary giants such as Henry Wadsworth Longfellow, who would remain a personal friend of Sumner long after the Bay State senator had alienated most of his other compatriots. Transcendentalism captured this optimism, in part individualistic, in part glorifying nature, in part a romantic's view of human relations; its writers and thinkers placed a value on humanity that was in many ways a contradiction of and, at the same time, a confirmation of traditional American values. Sumner embraced this movement while at the same time committing himself to the realm of radical reform politics that his friends abhorred.

Massachusetts did not see itself in isolation. Many of its people became committed reformers for perceived ills elsewhere. Akin to the zealousness of their Puritan forebears, they struck out to improve the world whether the world wanted to or not. While some pushed for the improvement of laboring conditions, others sought to create utopian communities like Brook Farm, many committed themselves to the compulsory school movement and teacher certification, while still others interested themselves in the reform of prisons. All of these movements combined in the push to abolish slavery. It was in this cause that Sumner found his true calling.

The abolitionist movement was not new to the English-speaking world when Sumner joined it in the late 1840s. Quakers in English North America—particularly in Quaker-founded Philadelphia, Pennsylvania—and England were at the forefront of societies that included such luminaries as Benjamin Franklin and Thomas Paine, author of *Common Sense* and propagandist extraordinaire. By the 1830s the abolitionists had made considerable progress. Britain had already ended her own African slave trade in 1807, devoted her navy to the cause after the Napoleonic Wars, and, finally, ended slavery in Britain and her colonies in 1833.

Less successful in the United States, the abolitionists could only secure a ban on the importation of slaves in 1808, largely with the help of native slaveholders desiring to increase the prices for their American-born slaves. Interestingly, the movement helped spur the nascent women's movement as the Grimké sisters, Angelina and Sarah, Lucretia Coffin Mott, and Elizabeth

Cady Stanton broke down barriers against women making speeches in public and participating in political debate. Denied entrance to the World Antislavery Convention in London in 1840, they and others later arranged the Seneca Falls Convention in 1848, founding the modern women's movement in the United States.

However, these paltry successes should not mislead one into thinking that abolitionism or abolitionists were popular in any way. In fact, for much of their history they and their cause were despised, ridiculed, frequently ignored, often banned, and sometimes violently suppressed. Two incidents illustrate the dangers. In the first in 1835, William Lloyd Garrison, fiery publisher of the abolitionist paper *The Liberator*, attempted to give a speech in Boston in place of the noted English abolitionist George Thompson. A crowd had gathered outside looking for Thompson. When informed of Thompson's absence, they turned on Garrison. The sheriff intervened and secured him from a certain lynching by placing him in jail.

The second incident took place in Alton, Illinois, on November 7, 1837. Elijah Lovejoy, a Presbyterian minister and publisher of the abolitionist paper the *Alton Observer*, decided to defend the fourth press he had brought into the unfriendly town. When a mob learned of the new arrival, they surrounded the warehouse where Lovejoy and his associates had decided to make their stand. While both sides exchanged gunfire, the mob placed a ladder against the building so they could set fire to the roof and burn the abolitionists out. When Lovejoy and others came out to push over the ladder a second time, he was shot five times and died shortly thereafter. The mob entered the building and destroyed the press, dumping the pieces into the Mississippi River. It was a strange scene considering that all Lovejoy was advocating was emancipation.

Emancipation, however, was extremely controversial. First of all, very few Americans believed African-Americans capable of being civilized members of society. Racism at this time was not only virulent but so accepted as to be pronounced as true in polite conversation, universities, and the halls of government. This feeling was no less prevalent in the free states of the Union than in the slave states. It is possible it was even stronger in the North as a result of the lack of exposure to African-Americans, as people often tend to fear and misunderstand what they do not know. Emancipation, it was feared, would lead to a migration of former slaves north. Most northern laborers were desperate to avoid such an invasion. Second, the abolitionists themselves did damage to their own cause through their stridency, moral superiority, and refusal to compromise on such a heated topic. Garrison epitomized this attitude when he burned and tore up the U.S. Constitution on a lecture hall stage because he believed it to be a proslavery document.

When Charles Sumner made abolitionism his cause in the late 1840s, it had already made substantial inroads into American politics, and its moralistic, self-righteous certitude fit him perfectly, for Sumner already demonstrated these qualities in spades. Returning from a trip to Europe a minor celebrity as a result of his associations with the leading lights and prominent social and political figures in Britain and elsewhere, he took up the practice of law and reform politics, socializing with the best people in Boston. Although he never succeeded at any of these activities, he did manage to enter the antislavery program at a critical moment. While many hoped the Missouri Compromise in 1820 had resolved the controversy about slavery in national politics, the admission of Texas to the Union in 1845 and the controversial war with Mexico that followed led to fears that slavery would expand into new territories, particularly when the gold rush in the newly acquired territory of California made the issue unavoidable.

Sumner belonged to the group of antislavery men in the Whig Party known as Conscience Whigs, but the Whig Party's leaders knew the danger of the slavery issue to their need to reconcile both Northerners and Southerners within their party if they were to have any chance of gaining the presidency. As a general policy, and with a more personal disregard to the obnoxious Sumner, they excluded him and the Conscience Whigs from high office. Sumner and his allies responded with the formation of their own political party, the aptly named Free Soil Party in 1848. Oddly enough, it was a coalition with Democrats under the maneuver called "fusion" that brought Sumner into contention for the Senate seat opened up upon Daniel Webster's resignation to become President Millard Fillmore's secretary of state. That prominent unionist had left the Senate under a cloud of acrimony when he made a speech supporting conciliation with the South in the form of what would become the Compromise of 1850. Although it took three months of balloting in the newly elected Massachusetts legislature, Sumner became a senator in 1851. There he would sit until his death in 1874, with the exception of his absences during his convalescence from the attack on May 22, 1856.

His assailant, Brooks, came from a very different world. South Carolina had welcomed slavery, embraced the slave trade, and made Africans and

"Charles Sumner" [between 1855 and 1865]. Brady-Handy Photograph Collection, Library of Congress Prints and Photographs Division, Washington, D.C.

African-Americans a majority of its population from the 1720s. Thus, South Carolina's history gave Brooks a starkly contrasting view of national and sectional politics, particularly on the issue of slavery. At least in part this was a result of plain-as-day demographics. In many respects his state was not just a slaveholding society, in which numbers of slaves worked alongside whites and shared in the dominant culture, but also a slave society, in which a minority of whites stood guard over a majority of slaves, deploying fierce laws and brutal punishments to control the slaves and ferret out any conspiracies before they could ripen. Through this extreme version of slavery, the society itself became the archetypal home to "the peculiar institution."

South Carolina owed this distinction to climate, geography, topography, and the acquisitive entrepreneurship of an able and alert planter class. Beginning its life in 1663 with Charles II's grant to eight proprietors, the Carolinas made up the future states of North Carolina and South Carolina. By the time the royal government split the colony in two in 1712, both had emerged from their tempestuous founding period. South Carolina was made up of two very different regions: the coastal plains marked by marshes and low-lying plains, hence the name low country, and the Piedmont region, which leads up to the Blue Ridge Mountains in the northwest, also known as the upcountry.

After several fits and starts with tobacco, cotton, indigo, and olives, the settlers, aided by their bondsmen, found the perfect crop for the tidal low lands: rice. Rice cultivation was backbreaking, labor-intensive work that required a substantial workforce organized in groups to maintain the irrigation ditches, weed the paddies, and harvest the crop. In China, Japan, India, Southeast Asia, and Africa, whole villages maintained and tended the crop. Carolina's settlers did not have such a ready supply of labor owing to the general unhealthiness of the area, which was buffeted during most of the year by malaria-carrying mosquitoes, typhus-infected waters, and other diseases. The colonists turned to African slaves to provide their workforce.

The horrors of the African slave trade are well documented. Packed onto ships from ports in West Africa, the Congo, or Angola, slaves went through the murderous "Middle Passage" across the Atlantic to arrive at the auction block in Charles Town, where they were inspected and sold, largely to sizable plantations where they experienced a death rate as high as or higher than the rest of the immigrant population. Working under torturous heat and humidity in the subtropical climate, Africans underwent a process of creolization. They adapted the widely varying ways of their homelands to their new environment. This syncretic culture enabled them to form extended families and social networks within and outside their plantation home. In South Carolina, most Africans worked alongside other Africans, allowing them to cling to African ways longer than slaves could in the North. The task system allowed them free time, but the patrol system prevented them from using that time to visit other plantations. They did manage to fish, hunt, and sell their labor to others when it was not required by their own masters.

A fierce set of laws imported from Barbados and gradually modified to fit South Carolina gave absolute power to masters. The slaves were technically chattel property like a horse or a chair, movable, valuable, but wholly under the control of their owners. Knowing that their slaves were also humans capable of sophisticated communication and actions, the master class set up what we might label a kind of police state. With the lessons learned from slave revolts elsewhere, as well as significant panics from slave disturbances such as Stono in 1739, whites developed a rigid classification system, slave patrols, a pass system, and forced illiteracy to keep their increasingly native slave population in line. While many skilled slaves managed to rise above their bondage to an extent, the vast majority were desperately impoverished, abused, and subject to the whims of their overseers and masters.

By the time of the American Revolution, South Carolina could boast a gentry and a society that was among the wealthiest in the English-speaking world and, thus, among the most prosperous on the planet. Like feudal lords of old, but with values and culture derived from Enlightenment Englishmen, the planter class, as well as the much larger group of farmers who owned only a few slaves, acted like, considered themselves to be, and expected to be treated as gentlemen. However, the South Carolina that constituted one of the leading states of the Union was not simply the rice plantations of the low country and the colonial capital and port of Charleston. South Carolina was much more diverse than that.

Besides the Huguenots (French Protestants), Sephardic Jews, Baptists, and Quakers, the proprietors' policy of religious toleration encouraged the immigration of a large number of Scots-Irish, who migrated into the upcountry from Virginia and Pennsylvania using the Great Wagon Road, a predecessor to the Appalachian Trail. The Scots-Irish were a fierce, bellicose people who populated the borderlands of the British Isles. At the time of their settlement of the Piedmont, they were Protestant, proud, and accustomed to the harsh life on the frontier. With their help, South Carolina forced the native Choctaw and Creek tribes out of the colony. However, they also participated along with their compatriots in North Carolina in the Regulator conflict that erupted in the 1760s, largely over representation in the state legislatures and the unequal distribution of power in favor of the large planters of the low country over the small-time farmers of the upcountry. The Revolution came slowly to the low country and split its planter class. The state that emerged gave disproportionate powers to the electors of the low country, even though the upcountry was filling with farmers.

The market revolution did not pass South Carolina by; like the rest of the country, her politics changed along with her economy. Possibly the most important transformation came about as the result of Eli Whitney's cotton gin. The compromises that effectuated the Constitution's three-fifths clause, the Bill of Rights, and, previously, the Northwest Territory agreements preventing slavery stemmed from the limits to rice and, more importantly, cotton planting. The long-staple cotton plant was easy to process but could not grow outside of the coasts. Thus, there was little concern at the end of the eighteenth century for the vast expansion of slavery to the upcountry and beyond. That changed with the popular adoption of Whitney's cotton gin, which could easily remove the sticky, green seeds from the short-staple cotton that could flourish inland. The massive bales of white, fluffy cotton found an almost insatiable demand in the mills of industrializing England and then those of England's competitors in New England and the Mid-Atlantic states.

With the expansion of the "cotton kingdom" came the further spread of plantation slavery. Increasingly the upcountry shared the slaveholding society of the low country. This drive for cotton profits expanded to the west, where the new southern states of Alabama, Mississippi, Arkansas, and Louisiana became populated by the Scots-Irish of South Carolina's upcountry, as well as other migrants from the Chesapeake. Rather than resent the spread of slavery that had driven them from their birthplaces, these transplants created their own slaveholding societies. The hope of becoming a plantation owner and, thus, part of the southern aristocracy salved any concerns they may have harbored about propagating a society based on the labor of people they alternately despised or feared depending on the circumstances.

In spite of the limiting nature of plantation slavery, throughout the rest of the antebellum period attitudes toward slavery's critics hardened. In part the motive was simply economic. Not only did slave states like South Carolina profit from slave labor, but much of the profit of cotton was reinvested in slave labor. The internal slave trade was a second benefit, and the production of new generations of slaves was a third. This confluence of self-interest and circumstance led to a direct collision with the prevailing attitudes of those in the free states who opposed slavery's expansion into the territories Northerners hoped to make their own.

Brooks's family lived in the upcountry, in the ninety-sixth electoral district of Edgefield County known as "Old 96." "Fighting Edgefield" became the center point for South Carolina politics as the population shifted to the interior. At the same time, more so than any other area in South Carolina, perhaps the entire South, this district gained a reputation for interpersonal violence. While in slavery itself violence hovered everywhere, the degree of violence among the ruling class was untoward. For part of the positive defense of slavery that southern intellectuals offered was that a slave society promoted harmony among the free. In a moral pamphlet, *The Devil in Petticoats*, about a wife who had killed three of her husbands, Parson Mason L. Weems, of George Washington biography fame, remarked: "Oh mercy! . . . Another murder in Edgefield. For sure it must be pandemonium itself, a very district of Devils!"[9]

Preston Brooks was born in Edgefield on August 5, 1819, in a substantial mansion surrounded by four acres of flower gardens. He was the second son of planter, lawyer, and politician Whitfield Brooks and Mary Carroll Brooks. His family connections crisscrossed the state, but with this prestige came the perils of a closely related, factional community. Young Preston did well in school and was intelligent, good-looking, and good-natured according to most accounts. After schooling at home, then at Moses Waddel's School in Willington, he attended South Carolina College, later renamed the University of South Carolina, in the state capital, Columbia. There he demonstrated the strong personality that colored his adult life. While a superb student, he was frequently absent. The taverns and social opportunities were too much of a temptation for this six-foot braggadocio. Altercations were frequent enough to gain notice.

Three episodes are worthy of description. After a disputed college election, he fought with a fellow student. Because he had refused to duel his opponent, he received only a temporary suspension while the other student was expelled. One might say that college boys, being privileged and recognized as gentlemen, often took to the field of honor. The second incident happened shortly before his expected graduation when Brooks heard that his brother had been arrested and jailed. With two pistols he broke into the jailhouse and demanded his brother's release. Disarmed without further incident, no charges were brought, but the College had had enough of his antics and withheld his degree.

A more serious encounter developed in 1840 when Louis T. Wigfall, a prominent rival of the Brooks family in Edgefield County politics, "posted" Whitfield Brooks for refusing to duel him. Posting was the last resort of an honor dispute with a recalcitrant opponent under the Code Duello. One put a sign in a public place denouncing the man in no uncertain terms. Per tradition, Wigfall also chose to defend the sign against removal. To be posted was one of the worst forms of shaming. Whitfield Brooks's brother-in-law, James Parsons Carroll, and another relative, Thomas Butler Bird, confronted Wigfall. In the pistol fight that ensued Bird died and Carroll challenged Wigfall to a duel. They met on Goat Island in the Savannah River to avoid falling under a legal jurisdiction that banned dueling. After an exchange of shots, their seconds convinced them honor had been satisfied.

But this was not satisfying to Brooks, who renewed the challenge. When their initial misses proved insufficient, Wigfall was shot through the thighs and Brooks in the hip in the second exchange. Both took time to recover, but Brooks emerged the victor, at least in public opinion. Negotiations over the various parties' newspaper publications continued after their respective recoveries. Eventually, a year after the original dispute had begun, both agreed to retractions of previous statements, and their seconds were credited with averting further violence. We should observe that despite the fact that dueling was illegal, no one would have thought to prosecute them for their behavior. In this community, there was a distinction between the letter of the law and actual sanctioned behavior. In cases of honor, social approbation sometimes came from setting aside the law books.

South Carolina, like other slave states, not to mention northern ones, passed anti-dueling laws, setting heavy fines for participation and ruling that in the case of a fatality, the charge was homicide. But seldom if ever were these penalties imposed. Legislatures would pass anti-dueling laws, but juries would never convict. The custom was too popular even though it meant that the upper caste of society was given the privilege of "natural liberty," that is, the right to challenge and fight under rules of the Code Duello, whereas ordinary citizens had to face the majesty of law.

However, Brooks did not act wholly according to his personal whim. Culture has a stickiness, an enveloping power that no one can entirely shed. Brooks wanted to be regarded by all in his community and state as a gentleman, wanted his father's and his older brother's and his neighbors' admiration, and to have acted otherwise in the Wigfall affair would have been to court shame. That state of existence carried far greater meaning than it does today. To be shamed meant to be considered an outcast of society, including one's own family perhaps, and to be forced to leave the region. Such a separation doomed the miscreant possibly to penury because he had no friends or family members to advance his fortune. In a society of low productivity and a limited number of professional positions of significance, that was a genuine hardship. It was this combination of personality and culture that almost dictated Brooks's actions. By submitting himself to the code, he showed his mettle as a man.

Brooks was less fortunate when it came time to prove his mettle in battle. He captained the all-volunteer Palmetto regiment in the Mexican War but had to leave for home when he developed debilitating typhus upon his entry on Mexican soil. In agony over his long recovery, seeing in his neighbors' faces disparaging looks, he managed to arrange for a regular army commission and sped to the front. Once there, he received a double blow: the death of his much-beloved older brother and the end of formal hostilities. With all of the fanfare of having served and none of the manful risks of combat, he returned home. He felt great shame in this set of circumstances.

It is no accident that the honor culture also prevailed in other societies that shared the slaveholding South's circumstances. With its aristocrats, large peasant population, and cultivated sense of superiority, France popularized its honor code through the presence of its officers among the revolutionaries in America's war for independence. Russia lost perhaps its greatest man of letters, Alexander Pushkin, in a duel. Germany was rife with young men who bore the scars of its form of duels with short sabers or had died from a thrust from a short sword. Duels were the natural outgrowth of the honor culture and the honor culture a natural outgrowth of an aristocratic society built on the oppression of a servile class.

In many respects, this was a transatlantic cultural phenomenon, an outgrowth of the Romantic movement. Besides reading Johann Wolfgang von Goethe's *The Sorrows of Young Werther*, gentlemen in all of these societies read the novels of authors such as Sir Walter Scott, which emphasized the knightly virtues of bygone eras. Oddly enough, Scott himself was a great opponent of dueling and the ethic of honor itself even though he romanticized the heroics of violent men. We also cannot discount the impact of religion, in particular Protestantism's emphasis on a sinful world and the inevitable temptations of man's passionate nature.

Despite the fact that South Carolina had outlawed the practice, as Brooks's

"Preston S. Brooks. Representative in Congress of the U.S. from South Carolina."
A. B. Walter engraver, H. Weber printer, C. Bohn publisher [ca. 1857]. Library of
Congress Prints and Photographs Division, Washington, D.C.

own history shows, features of the honor culture such as dueling remained
a part of South Carolinian life. Linked to one's public reputation, honor was
more than just manliness, character, and position in society. It undergirded
everything that made you who you were, from your credit-worthiness—a critical item in an economy built on debt—to your social life. Andrew Jackson
and Sam Houston had to flee their homes in South Carolina and Tennessee,
respectively, when their honor was impinged. For Jackson it was business

failures and allegations about his beloved wife; for Houston it was a mystery relating to his new wife. Because of its centrality to life in the South, and South Carolina especially, we cannot discount the honor culture's effect on every southern gentleman's worldview, including that of Preston S. Brooks.

Brooks had a well-established family life. Although his first wife died soon after the birth of their only child, he followed tradition and married her younger sister, with whom he had two more children. With the brief interruption of the Mexican-American War, he practiced law, managed a small plantation, and embarked on a career in politics. By 1852, when he ran for Congress in the fourth district, national politics had turned sour for defenders of the slaveholding South. England had ended slavery in its empire, and so had the French. The Royal Navy patrolled the African coast, intercepting slave traders. Latin American countries with the exception of Brazil had renounced slavery, although it still existed in portions of their old empire that the Spanish retained. More worrisome, at home abolitionists had redoubled their efforts, shifting from the effort to persuade slaveholders to free their slaves and provide for their passage to Africa to immediate emancipation in the states. The land gained from the Mexican War was not opened to slavery.

The inability to expand the realm of slavery was felt keenly in South Carolina. With no outlet for its black majority, many of the state's political leaders had developed a combative stance toward the slavery question. While a few moderates, such as Chief Justice John Belton O'Neal, urged confidence in the law and the Union, others became "fire-eaters" and demanded that some accommodation be made to South Carolina's needs or else. Whatever one's political stance in the state, South Carolina had taken on a Sparta-like quality by the early 1850s. All of her free white males were obligated to serve in the militia. Every man capable of bearing arms would have to gain a working knowledge of military affairs. When a master class is sitting on the powder keg of an enslaved African-American majority, they might well choose the Spartan solution to their enslaved helots: a commitment to the ways of soldiering and slave patrols.

This particular version of the social contract wedded the contradictory principles of limited government and the maintenance of a massive authority over the slaves. In the English-speaking world, the social contract took the form of laws that defined citizenship and the place of the citizen in this society. Although Brooks, like Sumner, gained admission to the bar and practiced for a brief time, his apprenticeship and his (not particularly impressive) role as an attorney in South Carolina were significantly different than they would have been in Massachusetts because of slavery. For example, Brooks had no opportunity to participate in a venture such as prison reform because there were no state penitentiaries in South Carolina and penal code reform became associated with abolitionism. For antebellum South Carolina the very concept of state-run penitentiaries for perpetual imprisonment was inimical. The prototypical criminal was the slave, devious in character, primitive in intellect, and prone to all the evils of a supposedly barbaric race under the philosophy that created race-based slavery. The slave system kept the animal nature of blacks in check.

Feeding into this siege mentality was South Carolina's unique experience in the Nullification Crisis from 1828 to March 1833. South Carolina had suffered enormously economically during the 1820s. Although it is likely that poor state planning, the financial collapse of 1819, and the rapidly depleted soils of the upcountry from cotton cultivation were the cause, an influential majority held the tariff—taxes on imports—the United States government passed in the 1820s, particularly the so-called Tariff of Abominations in 1828, responsible. Under the philosophical and legal reasoning of John C. Calhoun, Jackson's increasingly estranged vice president, South Carolina's legislature adopted the nullification doctrine as state policy in November of 1832, declaring that each state had a right under the U.S. Constitution to declare null and void federal legislation under certain conditions and that South Carolina was exercising that right regarding the tariff.

As Andrew Jackson was preparing to send the U.S. Navy to Charleston harbor to enforce federal law and South Carolina's governor prepared her militia, cooler heads in Washington, D.C., worked out a compromise. The Congress repealed the sections of the tariff law South Carolina opposed and passed a force bill authorizing President Jackson to use the U.S. military against South Carolina. When it became clear that even the leaders of Georgia and Alabama opposed her stance on nullification, South Carolina repealed her secession ordinance on March 11, 1833. Her leaders took several lessons from this crisis. First, South Carolina should not be caught unprepared militarily. Establishment of a military academy, later called the Citadel, in 1842 provided a future officer corps. Second, South Carolina should not act alone in any dispute over federal government powers. Third, the rest of the country preferred negotiation to war.

Another possible factor in South Carolina's stance during the 1850s stemmed from a development affecting the entire slaveholding South: the growing political and economic power of the North. From the time of the American Revolution, the opposite had been the case. Southerners had led the nation with only brief interruptions of southern-supported candidates or, in the case of John and John Quincy Adams, those presidents who had benefited from soon-to-disappear circumstances. John Adams inherited much of the support for George Washington, John Quincy that of James Monroe. This southern dominance stemmed from its vitality as the wealthiest section of the nation, its burgeoning population, and its leadership in military affairs.

Virginia and South Carolina were the sources of much of the settlers of the Upper South and Lower South, respectively, largely as a result of the erosion and depletion of the soil. In addition, Virginia supplied most of the population of the Lower Midwest as its poor white population migrated along the Ohio River into Ohio, Indiana, and Illinois. These migrants could not bring slaves, but they did bring southern culture and southern sympathies. When these populations combined with the southern-sympathizing populations of New Jersey, New York City, and Rhode Island, the South could very well think of herself as the mother of the nation.

Commerce too smiled on the South. The main system of transportation in the early nation was water-based, which depended on rivers that ran to the sea. The farmers of the Lower Midwest and the Upper South shipped their goods west and south along the Ohio and its tributaries to the Mississippi River and then to New Orleans. A large part of the purpose of Jefferson's Louisiana Purchase in 1803 was to ensure the navigability of what had become the nation's commercial highway. Financial, commercial, and other services developed to aid this flow. From the food served on the steamboats, to the slaves unloading and loading the cargo, to the blackface minstrels who performed in every steamboat's theater, all along the way people were reminded that America was a southern nation.

Last but not least, the military commands of the nation were entrusted to Southerners or their descendants. The tradition of an officer corps whose martial ardor was matched by their devotion to chivalric ways was embedded in the South. Although the cadet class at West Point—the nation's military academy—was distributed among the states, the officers who remained in the service for more than their required terms were more likely to be those whose southern orientation gave military service a high value. While the northern graduates disproportionately took the West Point engineering educations into private practice, the southern graduates sought higher command. It was no accident that they predominated in the army.

South Carolina could be proud of its pivotal role in the nation, and its leaders, such as John C. Calhoun, were at first stalwart nationalists. When he came to Congress from the upcountry in 1810, he supported internal improvements—national turnpikes and canals—as well as a protective tariff and a strong national military. But the balance of power between the sections, at first tilted to the South, began to change with the completion of the Erie Canal in 1825. It was not the first canal in the new nation—that honor went to the 1789 Richmond, Virginia, canal, to move barge traffic past the falls of the James River. However, the Erie Canal was a massive undertaking that reoriented the flow of agricultural and commercial traffic in the country. Some called it an eighth wonder of the world. It took eight years to build and thousands of workers, many of them Irish indentured servants, cutting their way through vast stands of original forest, sheer rock, and pestilential swamps. It required eighty-three locks—an engineering device that allowed for the counter-raising and lowering of offsetting pools of water—to traverse the over 360 miles and staggering ascent and descent of 680 feet from Albany on the Hudson River to Buffalo on the opposite side of New York State on Lake Erie.

A mere decade after its completion, shipping along its course cost a tenth of the overland haulage and provided an alternative to the Mississippi River route. This ignited a boom in the transfer of goods and people from New York City to Albany, Buffalo, and the interior of the Upper Midwest all along the Great Lakes that linked those regions to the canal. Besides spawning a splurge of canal construction throughout the country, it knitted the Upper Midwest to the Northeast economically and demographically. It funded New York City banking and stock trading and provided capital for the New England and Middle Atlantic states' industry. It left South Carolina out, reinforcing economically and then psychologically the state's sense of isolation. By the late 1820s, Calhoun was no longer a nationalist. He had become the most forceful and implacable advocate of states rights, the untouchability of slavery, and the privilege of a state to nullify federal laws.

With the opening of economic opportunity all along the Erie Canal, the region drew masses of immigrants from abroad. Germans, Scandinavians, and, in a tremendous wave after the Potato Famine of 1845, the Irish fled their homelands—wracked by war, want, and political oppression, and sometimes a combination of all three—for the United States. Although the shipping companies' promises of cities with streets paved with gold were obviously exaggerations, the economic opportunity in the North was sufficiently tempting to bring tens of thousands of these immigrants into Boston and New York, along the canals or the developing railroads, and eventually into the towns carved out of the wilderness. The boosters of these towns encouraged the influx of immigrants, as well as the canals and railroads they hoped would enhance the prosperity of the region. While many civic leaders would be disappointed when the prosperity failed to materialize, for the unstable economics of boom meant that busts were never far away, the free labor states of the North became the nation's most populous area.

No one personified this transformation of the nation into sections—and its inherent tensions—more than one of the bystanders to the caning of Charles Sumner, his frequent opponent Senator Stephen A. Douglas of Illinois. He was known as the "Little Giant" for his diminutive stature—only five feet two inches tall and under a hundred pounds—and his contrastingly large head, broad shoulders, and forceful speaking style. He was a New Englander by birth who had fled his native Vermont for the opportunities in the West. He adopted Illinois as his home and viewed himself as a westerner thereafter. However, despite his home in Chicago, his was not the Illinois of transplanted New Englanders, but the southern-leaning prairies of southern Illinois. After an unsuccessful courting of Mary Todd, who chose Abraham Lincoln instead, the successful attorney married another southern belle, Martha Martin, whose Mississippi plantation brought him wealth and many slaves to manage. What would have been a natural sympathy toward the slaveholding South was now a personal, financial, and family matter.

As a successful attorney, Democrat, and advocate for the principles of the party of Jackson, his rise to the top of Illinois politics was rapid to the point of meteoric. From county attorney he became a state legislator, Illinois secretary of state, and, in 1841 at twenty-seven, an associate justice of the Illinois Supreme Court. In 1843 he began his distinguished career in Congress with two terms as a representative; then, in 1847, he became a senator. He gained repute as a debater, a master of the legislative process, and a supreme manipulator of coalition politics while at the same time advancing the interests of his state, section, and party, which he believed coalesced in expansion west.

By 1850, he became chair of the Senate Committee on the Territories, the focus for almost all of the contentious issues of that tumultuous decade.

While no avid defender of African-American slavery, Douglas despised the abolitionists and their cause. For him those attempting to interfere with the South's peculiar institution were at best misguided, at worst troublemaking malcontents who did not understand how American democracy worked. He believed in compromise out of both personal conviction and political expediency. This consummate politician had a thirst for advancement few could match. Ultimately, he saw himself as the standard bearer of the Democratic Party, but he needed to subdue the pesky slavery extension issue first.

For Douglas to gain his great goal, the presidency, he and his party would have to stand astride the sectional divide. For Massachusetts and South Carolina had not yet come to blows. He might yet find votes in both states, a delicate balancing act. Brooks and Sumner might be irreconcilable, but the moderates on both sides might be persuaded to compromise. It had happened before, but only after fulminations and bluster brought Congress to near paralysis. The problem was what to do with Douglas's adopted region, the West, when proslavery and free-soil forces contested the expansion of the peculiar institution.

Although their paths to prominence were as different as their backgrounds, these three men shared many things besides their careers as lawyers, politicians, and Americans. They each, in their own way, represented their respective states and sections. Their disagreements stemmed from matters of principle as well as practical politics and economic interests. While Brooks emphasized honor and Sumner idealism, they both rejected Douglas's attempt at a third way. Geography may or may not be destiny, but it found its avatars in the clash of worldviews Brooks, Sumner, and Douglas brought with them to the Capitol.

2 } A MACHINE THAT WOULD GO OF ITSELF?

IN 1986, Michael Kammen titled his prize-winning book on common understandings of the U.S. Constitution *A Machine That Would Go of Itself*. The line itself is from a James Russell Lowell essay on the workings of American government: "it seemed as if we had invented a machine that would go of itself." However, Lowell wrote in 1888 and rued the offhanded faith in the Union that Americans shared before the Civil War. If the Constitution were indeed such a machine, needing little human intervention, then the project of federalism would be safe. Disputes over slavery could not wreck the mechanism of American self-government or undo the Union.

Although Americans liked to think of their basic law as immutable and working automatically without prejudice or favor, national politics in action belied that expectation. Rather than a machine, the best metaphor would be a boxing match without an official. It had rules, but the fighters were charged with its enforcement, with the ultimate authority about the cleanliness of the match left to the crowd. This reality came about through two main factors: the framing of the Constitution and subsequent developments, which laid bare its deficiencies, nuances, and the difficulties inherent in governing any country like the United States.

A work of compromise and, on occasion, deliberate vagueness, the U.S. Constitution had several major deficiencies when it came to putting its provisions into practice. For one, it did not anticipate the formation or the durability of a two-party system. Coupled with the laxity of the provisions for the Electoral College (the candidate with the majority of the electors' votes was to be president, the second vote getter to be vice president), the early and fierce rise of the two-party system led directly to the disputed election of 1800. Aaron Burr, who was supposed to be the Republicans' vice presidential candidate, tied Thomas Jefferson, the presidential nominee, in the Electoral College. Thankfully for future generations, an amendment took care of that situation, but no amendment could be wide ranging enough to mitigate the effects of partisan competition on the behavior of candidates, much less the elected officials.

The second major flaw in the Constitution was that it compromised on the nature of the Union it formed. Major questions of federalism went unanswered. Although there was a supremacy clause, it only applied to so-called enumerated powers explicitly given to the federal or national government. Combined with the subsequently ratified Ninth and Tenth Amendments, the vagueness of the government's powers with respect to that of the states remained to bedevil subsequent generations. When Thomas Jefferson and James Madison penned the Kentucky and Virginia Resolutions in response to the Sedition Act crisis of the John Adams administration, two of the nation's preeminent founding fathers and future presidents gave their prestige to a set of arguments that their political heirs would use to advocate interposition, nullification, and ultimately secession. Namely, those resolves verged on describing the Union as a compact among sovereign states instead of an indissoluble agreement to form a national government.

Finally, poor draftsmanship and the magisterial desire to compromise over vast fissures in the populace about issues such as slavery left behind a minefield for future generations to navigate, particularly with regard to the admission of new areas to the country. Although Congress received explicit powers over the territories of the United States and the procedure for admitting new states was clear enough, the question of slavery's expansion into those territories was unresolved.

After all, slavery existed in several realms simultaneously. The Constitution alluded to "other persons" frequently and, at one point, in the so-called Rendition Clause, empowered the national government to enforce and enact a Fugitive Slave Law. The Bill of Rights, which amended the original document soon after the formation of its first government, also provided an explicit protection for property, and where it existed, slavery was a species of property law. At the same time, slavery was a creation of state or "municipal" law. Thus, it could exist in one state but be banned in another. The so-called Comity Clause of the Constitution commanded that all states give "full faith and credit" to the "the public Acts, Records, and judicial Proceedings of every other State," but what if those laws clashed as they did on slavery? The question was a staple of a well-established area of law called "conflict of laws," but the legal literature of the time afforded no clear answer. Indeed, the foremost jurists of the time, including Supreme Court Justice Joseph Story and New York's Chancellor James Kent, had wrestled with it and been pinned.

These three major problems in the body of the Constitution—its neglect of partisan impulses and excesses in American politics, its incompleteness on the subject of federal-state relations, and its uneasy compromises over slavery—interacted in dangerous ways as the people and the politicians of the free states and slave states clashed over whether slavery should expand into new territories. The issue did not emerge virulently with regard to the Northwest Territory and the old Southwest because those areas offset one another, the South was dominant in national affairs, and the fate of those regions rested on deals made during the confederation period prior to the Constitution's ratification. The Northwest Territory and the states carved from it were not to have slavery. No barrier was to be erected against slavery in the Southwest, opening its doors to the expansion of the peculiar institution.

The Problem of Slavery

The first strident debate in Congress over the expansion of slavery exploded during the closing years of the so-called Era of Good Feelings (1816–24), when James Monroe's Union Republicans were everywhere triumphant and willing to make concessions to their defeated foes in a spirit of magnanimity. When it did erupt, it began a long, fractious, and complicated contest over the expansion of slavery into which the Brooks-Sumner affair fit.

In 1819 slavery's advocates desired the admission of Missouri, which already had a fair number of slaves owing to its common border along the Mississippi River with the slave states of Kentucky and Tennessee. Northerners objected. James Talmadge, a New York congressman, proposed an amendment to the Missouri statehood bill "that further introduction of slavery or involuntary servitude be prohibited and that all children of slaves born within the said state after the admission thereof into the Union shall be free." The South's representatives objected to the admission of the Maine Territory, previously a possession of Massachusetts, as a state. Because the admission of one would offset the addition of the other, preserving the perfect balance between nominal slave states (Delaware had few slaves but voted with the South anyway) and free states in the Senate, a great compromise was possible. Conceding that slavery was unlikely in the area to the west and north of Missouri beyond her southern border on latitude line thirty-six degrees, thirty minutes, the Congress also prohibited slavery north of that line. Thus, the Missouri Compromise became law in 1820–21.

Left behind in this spirit of conciliation were the gnawing uncertainties surrounding such an assertion of lawmaking power. How could Congress strip slave property from its owners by declaring their domicile free of slavery? Why should free states accept a balance in the government that masked southern dominance when the majority of the nation's population lived in free states? What would be the outcome of territorial acquisitions to the west of the Louisiana Purchase should further territory be acquired? Would both sides be as accommodating in a more divisive environment? During the debates on Missouri, some Southerners had threatened disunion if slavery were prohibited. Georgia's Thomas W. Cobb declared that prohibition of slavery would "have kindled a fire which . . . seas of blood can only extinguish."[1] The nation would have to answer these questions as the Era of Good Feelings broke apart in the election of 1824, a mere eight years after it had begun.

The immediate cause of the trouble that led to Charles Sumner's "Crime against Kansas" speech began with the annexation of the Republic of Texas. Although the Alamo receives attention in film and legend, the end of the struggle between the rebelling Texans and the Mexican army took place at the Battle of San Jacinto on April 21, 1836. Sam Houston, having escaped the perils of caning congressmen in Washington, D.C., outgeneraled Mexican dictator Antonio Lopez de Santa Anna. Santa Anna himself was captured, having fled in disguise from the disaster, and was forced to sign a treaty recognizing the independence of the Lone Star Republic. Stephen F. Austin established his government in the city that bore his name and bequeathed to his successor, Houston, a slaveholding republic with a mountain of debt and a lingering dispute with Mexico, which had since overthrown Santa Anna and disavowed the treaty he had signed.

The dispute was over whether the republic's border was the Nueces River— the boundary of the original Mexican province of Tejas—or the Rio Grande, as much as two hundred miles to the south. The dispute also included Mexican possessions to the west, encompassing much of present-day New Mexico, including Santa Fe. Knowing that the only real solution to the debt problem lay with admission to the United States under an arrangement whereby the federal government would assume the debt of the former republic, Texan leaders applied for admission as a slave state.

The Texas issue became the issue uniting and dividing segments of both the Democratic and Whig Parties. Both parties were desperate for a solution that would appeal to their members and potential swing voters in both sections. This was not an easy task as both parties were made up of not only coalitions that were divided by whether they hailed from the North and were opposed to slavery extension or from the South and supported slavery extension, but also factions that had formed around various leaders, around previous controversies, and, on occasion, on policy.

The eventual Whig Party nominee for president in 1844 was Henry Clay, whose quest for that high office had twice before ended in failure. Clay had first stepped onto the national stage at the ripe old age of thirty-three when, in his first term as a congressman, he became Speaker of the House. Perhaps his few years in the Senate prior to the House helped. In the six Congresses in which he served as Speaker, he turned it into the second most powerful position in the government, a position it has sustained ever since. Many credit this great advocate of the western states with the War of 1812, as well as the formation of the Whig Party and its commitment to tariffs, infrastructure improvements, and hard money that formed what Clay called "The American System."

But the Kentuckian now hit on a theme that he hoped would unify his party and garner national appeal: the no-territory pledge. Why not just avoid the fractious issue of slavery extension altogether by not acquiring any more territory? Clay and the Whigs could claim that they were putting nation ahead of section while simultaneously satisfying both North and South by avoiding the question. Unfortunately for Clay and the Whigs, John Tyler had other ideas.

The Whigs had placed Tyler, a slaveholder from Virginia, on the bottom half of their presidential ticket in 1840 in order to provide sectional balance. The ticket leader was William Henry Harrison, the victor of the Battle of Tippecanoe on November 7, 1811. The ticket that gave the nation the campaign slogan of "Tippecanoe and Tyler Too!" triumphed over the extremely unpopular Democrat Van Buren, who had the misfortune of following Andrew Jackson into one of the worst economic downturns in U.S. history. Setting a precedent for Whig presidents, Harrison died soon after taking the oath of office. The general had insisted on giving his inaugural address in a rainstorm. His cold transformed into a lethal pneumonia, which carried him off on April 4, 1841, a scant few weeks into his term. Tyler, the first vice president to succeed to the office of president—"his accidency" his opponents called him—decided to abandon the Whig program of tariffs, internal improvements, and deference to Congress and instead favor the limited government and more expansionist-leaning preferences of the Democrats.

As for the Democrats, they were ready to live up to the Will Rogers joke of the early twentieth century: "I am not a member of any organized political party. I am a Democrat." In addition to the usual sectional division, they now had to overcome the challenge of a divided New York delegation. The so-called Barnburners backed Van Buren, who was opposed to Texas annexation and favored limiting the spread of slavery. Their opponents called them Barnburners because someone who burned down their barn to eliminate a rat infestation was destroying the building in order to save it, just as a Democrat seeking to talk about slavery would destroy the Democratic Party in order to save it. In turn, the Barnburners' rivals in New York were called Hunker Democrats because they hankered or hunkered after offices only an alliance with southern Democrats could produce. Making Van Buren's nomination virtually impossible was the southern Democrats and Hunkers' imposition of a two-thirds rule for a candidate to receive the nomination for president. Two-thirds of the delegates would be an insurmountable barrier except for one who had the support of the South.

Because of these divisions, the Democrats stalemated the national party convention until a dark-horse candidate emerged who promised to serve both wings of the party. James K. Polk was Jackson's heir in Tennessee after Sam Houston's sudden departure. Although distasteful to the Barnburners for his slaveholding and desire to expand U.S. territory to the Pacific, he promised the remaining northern Democrats that he would secure the whole of the Oregon Territory, an area unlikely for slavery owing to a climate inhospitable to any of plantation slavery's traditional crops. Polk pledged himself to annexation and possible war with Mexico, if that event came to pass, and Polk had every intention of finding an excuse to start that war.

Clay fumbled the election when, nervous about Polk's pledge to secure Oregon, he wrote a public letter confessing he had no personal objection to annexation. This seeming waffling on the critical issue of expansion weakened his candidacy. The abolitionists under the Liberty Party banner selected a southern former slaveholder who had converted to abolitionism, James G. Birney, as their nominee for president. He showed no such qualms about slavery's expansion. It is likely that Clay's letter cost him the thirty-five thousand votes to Birney that Clay needed in order to beat Polk in New York— throwing the state and the presidency to Polk.

Polk need not have worried about jamming Texas down Congress's throat. The lame duck Tyler had already performed that operation. After the Whigs in the Senate combined with their Barnburner allies to defeat the treaty for Texas annexation by denying the two-thirds majority it needed for ratification, Tyler arranged for the dubious maneuver of a joint resolution admitting Texas as a state from the slim Democratic majorities in both houses. Texas— immense, slaveholding, debt-ridden, and in a dispute with Mexico—became part of the United States and brought with it all of its problems.

Polk still had his date with manifest destiny. His overriding desire for expansion now sought a new outlet: California, a Mexican province encompassing not only the present-day state of California but also Nevada, Arizona, Colorado, and western New Mexico. In order to avoid a two-front war, Polk adopted an aggressive negotiating strategy with Britain. He threatened to make war over the entire Oregon Territory (the popular Democratic cry of "Fifty-Four Forty or Fight!" claiming the uppermost latitude line defining the area). Polk had little hope of success in this endeavor. Prime Minister Robert Peel and his foreign secretary, the Earl of Aberdeen, could wield naval forces more than capable of devastating the eastern seaboard and the Great Lakes. At the same time, the Irish famine caused a greater than usual English dependence on American wheat and corn, while tensions on the European continent centered on a new Napoleon, Napoleon III, taking power in France.

Polk's own party was stoking war fever. John L. O'Sullivan, editor of the *New York Morning News*, summed up the Democratic mood when he wrote that the United States had a right to Oregon "by right of our manifest destiny to overspread and possess the whole of the continent." But moderates soon acceded to the wisdom of avoiding a conflict over a remote land that was too sparsely populated for it to be worth waging another war with Britain. On June 18, 1846, the Senate ratified a compromise treaty with Britain, which set the boundary in the middle of Oregon at the forty-ninth parallel.

Besides, Polk had more pressing matters with which to deal. By that time, the United States had officially been at war with Mexico for a little over a month. While Washington, Adams, Jefferson, and even Jackson had used diplomacy to avoid entangling foreign wars, Polk's machinations made war with Mexico inevitable. When Mexico predictably turned down his offer to purchase the territory, Polk ordered U.S. troops to the disputed boundary on the Rio Grande. After the expected exchange of gunfire between Mexican troops patrolling the area and what the Mexicans perceived as the invading forces of the United States, Polk informed the Congress that Mexico had fired on and killed U.S. soldiers. Two days later, on May 13, 1846, Congress declared war.

Polk hardly anticipated the scope and expense of the war that resulted, costing thirteen thousand American lives and nearly one hundred million dollars. As a Democrat, he favored a weak central government and budget stringency. More likely, he was engaging in aggressive negotiations. Instead, a revolving-door Mexican ministry, relying on its own concept of honor, refused to cede any part of its territory to the United States. Only after a year and nine months of prolonged combat operations over thousands of miles of land and by sea that culminated in the seizure of Mexico City did Polk achieve his goal. His health suffered to the point where he decided he could not seek another term, and domestic opposition against his "war for slavery" reached unheard-of levels. The result was as he had wished: the Mexican cession increased the United States by a third, and the nation now commanded several thousand miles of Pacific coastline—initiating more than a decade-long struggle over slavery's extension.

Even before U.S. forces had begun their long march to Mexico City, David Wilmot, a Democrat from Pennsylvania, sought to take the slavery expansion question out of the national debate by arranging for a congressional agreement that slavery would be barred from any territories gained from Mexico. Known as the Wilmot Proviso, instead of lessening tensions, Wilmot's plan exacerbated them. Favoring the Wilmot Proviso became the litmus test for northern Democrats and a death sentence for the careers of southern Democrats.

Polk contributed to the sectional wrangling when he advocated that Texas's boundary be the Rio Grande in the west as well as the south, an additional swath of territory for slavery comprising present-day eastern New Mexico and its future capital Santa Fe. Muddying the waters even further, he made himself a lame-duck president by pledging not to seek a second term. Finally, he made the news official that gold had been discovered at Sutter's Mill in northern California across the bay from San Francisco. This touched off the massive California gold rush the following year, 1849, in which Americans and Europeans set off in one of the world's largest modern mass migrations. California's population began to surge well past the U.S. Army's capability to control it. Its residents begged for a government.

As a result, the pro-slavery-expansion and anti-slavery-expansion forces waged combat with one another over another presidential and congressional election. Owing to the lack of uniformity in the timing of these separate elections, a lame-duck Congress would have a whack at the issue before giving way to a partially new Congress that would then have a new president, and then, finally, an entirely new Congress would deal with a new president before the campaign for a new Congress in 1850 began. This constant campaigning for office spurred the parties to maneuver for advantage rather than take the time to coolly consider the crafting of a comprehensive solution.

Popular Sovereignty and Fugitive Slaves

There was also the matter of the assumptions that drove the politics in this period. Nowhere was the power of these assumptions more prevalent than in the presidential campaign of 1848. The Democratic nomination went to Michigan's Lewis Cass, much to the consternation of Van Buren's pro–Wilmot Proviso forces. Despite his roots in the North, Cass had adopted the political doctrine of "popular sovereignty" to resolve the question of slavery in the territories. In many respects it was the perfect solution. Instead of Congress having to decide the issue, it could pass on the responsibility to the territories.

Popular sovereignty sounded democratic principles, and it could be sold in two very different ways: one for the North, and one for the South. Democrats told Northerners that Northerners would populate the western territories because the climate was inhospitable to plantation slavery. Once enough people entered into a territory, they would form a territorial legislature banning slavery. Democrats told Southerners that the moment when a territory applied for statehood with a constitution would be the time the status of slavery would be decided. They could take comfort from the fact that no territory with any slaves had applied for statehood with an antislavery constitution.

Besides being two-faced about an issue of critical importance to their constituents, Cass's policy assumed a great deal about slavery. First, the link between climate and slavery was anything but assured. After all, much of

"General Map of the United States, showing the area and extent of the free & slave-holding states, and the territories of the Union." Engraved by W. & A. K. Johnston, Edinburgh [1857]. Library of Congress Geography and Map Division, Washington, D.C.

Missouri was the same latitude as the southern Midwest, and slavery did not go into the Midwest only because of the prohibition of the Northwest Ordinances. Furthermore, in Virginia, Kentucky, and other places unsuitable for cotton and dead to tobacco, slaves were used in the wheat, corn, and other grain fields, as well as for tending hogs, chickens, and cattle. In Virginia slaves were increasingly employed in small industry. In Maryland they were employed in shipbuilding. There was no reason slave labor could not have effectively competed with free labor wherever slaves' masters might take them.

Second, both sides of the debate predicted that free states would vote along with other free states against slavery. More extreme thinkers such as Calhoun and Alabama's Senator William Lowndes Yancey refused to accept any limits on slaveholders' rights. They not only denounced popular sovereignty but also refused any accommodation with Northerners over the slavery issue. These so-called fire-eaters foresaw the end of slavery if it did not receive explicit protection from the national government. This protection would not be forthcoming if free states outnumbered slave states. They even openly declared that they would pursue secession from the Union if slavery was interfered with in any way.

This position is difficult to understand if viewed as a matter of purely constitutional law. The abolition of slavery in the South would require a constitutional amendment in order to get around the compensation problem the Fifth Amendment created with its guarantees of due process and fair compensation for private property taken by the government. Even had Congress the will to take slaves by eminent domain, the cost would have been astronomical. An amendment needed three-fourths of the states in addition to two-thirds of both houses of Congress or two-thirds of the legislatures of the states proposing a convention in order to change the Constitution. With the admission of Texas and Florida in 1846, there were fifteen slave states, including Delaware. Based on that number, there would have to be sixty states in the Union and forty-five of them would have to agree to abolish slavery. Not only was this scenario unlikely, but it would be impossible if the slave states refused to allow the admission of the requisite number of free states. Only if the slave states managed to put themselves into a position where Congress would be able to force them to adopt such an amendment would this dire threat become a reality. It is one of the great ironies of history that the fire-eaters' efforts accomplished this very task by 1865.

Whatever might have been the outcome of this hypothetical reasoning, the Democrats and Cass were unlucky enough to run up against a Whig Party that was even more effective in burying the slavery extension issue. Their nomination went to the Louisiana slaveholder and Mexican-American War hero Zachary Taylor, whose political affiliations were so quiet that the Democrats and the Whigs had assurances he was one of them up until the nominating conventions. Despite the fact that Barnburners and Conscience Whigs were so unhappy with their respective party's candidate that they joined with the Liberty Party to form the Free Soil Party and run Van Buren, Taylor's pledge to respect the will of Congress in all matters defeated Cass and popular sovereignty. Cass was unable to convince Southerners he would bow to their interests and Northerners that he was not beholden to the South.

But Whig celebrations did not last long. Their legislative hopes suffered a significant blow between Taylor's victory and the congressional races in 1849. In January of that year, reacting to the Northerners' proposal to ban the slave trade in Washington, D.C., Calhoun called for a caucus—a gathering to organize for the upcoming session—of the South's delegation and gave the Democrats who attended, Whigs being absent from a call so dangerous to their party, what he later published as his "Southern Address." In effect both a legal brief and a political statement, it laid out the northern assaults on southern liberties, linked them to violated guarantees of the Constitution, and declared any compromise on slavery to be a betrayal of the region and the fundamental law. By denying southern states their equal status in the compact between sovereign states that was the Constitution, the North was trying to "sink them, from being equals, into a subordinate and dependent condition."[2] The obvious conclusion was that if the South was not treated appropriately—that is, given the right to expand slavery into the whole of U.S. territory—the slave states had to secede from the United States for their own protection.

While Whigs studiously avoided this very Democratic plea for southern unity, the Southern Address gained potency from President Zachary Taylor's presidential address, which proposed the immediate admission of California as a free state. Fearing encirclement, southern voters gutted the Whig Party in the South. Interestingly enough, when California heeded Taylor's call to form a state government, California sent both a free-state constitution and two Democratic senators to the Congress. But Calhoun's argument was still persuasive to southern Democrats because any prohibition on slavery violated their conception of the federative compact. Stuck between the hard place of Calhoun's belligerence and the rock of Taylor's intransigence, Congress stalemated. Then Clay took the floor.

With his glory days well behind him, Kentucky reelected him a senator for the third time in 1849. In 1850, he made a final contribution to the national unity he dedicated his political life to forging. On January 29, 1850, Clay addressed the Senate endorsing a compromise. Although none of his specific proposals became law, his notion of a series of bills satisfying to a coalition in both the North and South began the process of reconciliation.

Thankfully for the Union, a Mississippi- and Tennessee-arranged convention in Nashville did not produce ordinances of secession from the Lower South—only the threat of secession if the South was not conciliated. It is important to note that very few Northerners and unionist politicians denounced this gathering or the concept that a state or states could remove themselves from the nation. What could conceivably be regarded as treason—the sundering of the United States—was treated instead as a political matter, which required tact and conciliation to solve. It was an ominous precedent.

The matters under debate in Clay's proposal were the admission of California, the western border of Texas, what to do with the territories in between, and the South's demand for the more effective Fugitive Slave Law that Virginia Senator James M. Mason wrote. Taylor and Clay insisted on an omnibus bill—a conglomeration of all of the elements into one piece of legislation— but this prevented any wiggle room for cross-sectional and cross-party alliances. Northern Whig legislators could not vote for the popular sovereignty provisions for the territories. Southern Whigs and Democrats could not vote for the admission of California. Northern Democrats would be hard-pressed to vote for a larger Texas.

When the omnibus bill went down to defeat, Democrats gleefully celebrated their victory over the Whig Party. But they gained that victory at considerable cost. The debates had become so acrimonious that, at one point, Senator Henry S. Foote of Mississippi pulled out a gun and pointed it at Missouri's Thomas Hart Benton—and both men were Democrats. In the meantime, the conflict over what to do with Santa Fe between the Texas state government and the national government threatened to turn into a shooting war. Taylor contributed to the controversy when he came down solidly on bringing the Texas state militia to heel by force if necessary. Compromise on any part of the issue of the Mexican cession seemed remote at best.

However, as an ill fate would have it, Taylor left the presidency in similar fashion to Harrison. After eating a bowl of cherries and cream in the hot sun of a July Fourth celebration, he came down with a fatal case of gastrointestinal distress. On July 9, 1850, his vice president, Millard Fillmore, became president. Disagreeing with Taylor's controversial picks for federal jobs, he and Daniel Webster used the presidential patronage power to persuade recalcitrant Whigs to vote in favor of compromise. Webster had already alienated the anti-slavery-expansion North with his speech on March 7, pleading for unity and explicitly endorsing Mason's fugitive slave bill. He opened, "I wish to speak today, not as a Massachusetts man, nor as a Northern man, but as an American, and a member of the Senate of the United States."[3] He declared the North's triumph unassailable. Therefore, it could afford to be conciliatory toward the South. Excoriated in the North, Webster resigned from the Senate to become Fillmore's secretary of state. There he helped Fillmore back the more effective strategy of Stephen Douglas.

Douglas decided to unbundle the proposals. That way Northerners and Southerners could vote yes on one measure while voting no on others, or, better yet, not vote at all. With Fillmore and Webster wielding the stick of federal job appointments over Whigs, Douglas could work with coalitions of Democrats on individual bills. However, with his margins extremely thin and his presidential ambitions combining with his desire to placate the South to maintain Democratic unity, he chose popular sovereignty as the solution for the Utah and New Mexico Territory bills. It was a decision consistent with his commitment since boyhood to Jacksonian Democracy. Thus, popular sovereignty became the law of the land over the objections of both the Free-Soilers and fire-eaters. In the meantime, much of the fire had gone out of the controversy. With the death of Calhoun on March 31, 1850, the passage of the Fugitive Slave Law, the admission of California, and a reduced boundary of Texas (leaving the New Mexico Territory to be organized later), the so-called Compromise of 1850 received Fillmore's signature and appeared to quiet the slavery controversy.

Even the state conventions in Mississippi, South Carolina, Georgia, and Alabama held in June lost their secessionist fervor to the new spirit of unity the Compromise of 1850 spawned. Unionist-minded Whigs Robert Toombs, Alexander Stephens, and Howell Cobb were able to forge a moderate Georgia Platform, which Alabama's and Mississippi's conventions adopted, endorsing the Compromise of 1850 as the permanent settlement of the slavery question. The state elections of 1851 confirmed the unionist Whigs in this stand, but there were ominous signs that belied this feeling of unity.

First and foremost was the fact that the Compromise of 1850 was not actually a compromise at all. The two sections did not agree on any portion of it. Douglas's majorities were largely sectional and only succeeded with slight defections and nonvoting. Second, when Fillmore revealed his opposition to Texas Governor John Bell's threat to march on Santa Fe in the midst of the crisis over the compromise, there were calls throughout the South to raise forces to aid the Texans in their struggle with the United States.

Third, even the Georgia Platform endorsed secession as a last resort if the rights of the South were attacked by the national government, a threat that might be fulfilled at any moment Southerners felt sufficiently aggrieved. That these threats were ignored by federal law enforcement officials again bespoke a tolerance for such threats, or rather, they were regarded as mere political oratory. Inasmuch as both threats were contrary to the laws of the United States, the fact that they were not denounced by anyone in authority indulged their authors' fiery orations and secessionist impulses.

The long-term benefits of the Compromise of 1850 rested with the Democrats. The Whig Party in the North was badly fractured. Besides the wrangling between the Fillmore loyalists and the Conscience Whig forces, there was the fact that Whigs could no longer wage a campaign on either the slavery issue or the economy. Pledged to the support of all of the compromise, Whigs were caught in the middle of the firestorm that arose around the Fugitive Slave Law of 1850.

Mason's law had several provisions strengthening federal power and offending free soil. The irony was that Southerners, in particular southern Democrats, opposed a strong central government. But the Fugitive Slave Law of 1850 introduced bench trials that forbade the alleged fugitive from testifying and compulsory enforcement provisions falling on everyone summoned to convey the alleged slave southward. If turning every citizen in the North into a slave catcher was not enough, there was the fact that northern states' laws prohibiting the existence of slavery counted for nothing. Northern legislatures roused from their slumber responded with "personal liberty laws" designed to interpose state officials between black residents of the state and federal commissioners, and, on occasion, mobs attempted to thwart federal officials from carrying out federal law extraditing African-Americans to the South. In effect, northern states edged toward the nullification doctrines that southern states had pioneered.

However, the compromise held, with so much depending on it that even the party that had brokered the deal, the Whigs, could not benefit from it in the election of 1852. Ironically, the weakness in the party that the compromise revealed led to the smashing Electoral College victory of New Hampshire Democrat Franklin Pierce. In this setting of uneasy peace, it seemed that only a catastrophic error could reopen the debate over slavery extension. Precisely because he sought to gain the presidency in 1856, it was Stephen A. Douglas, the true author of the Compromise of 1850, who unmade the uneasy peace.

Ever since Douglas arranged for his committee on the territories to report out what became the Kansas-Nebraska Act, people have wondered what motivated him to reopen the slavery extension issue. By proposing to apply the popular sovereignty doctrine to territory made free by the Missouri Compromise line, he reopened the scar tissue of the Missouri crisis. One may surmise his motivation. He owned land along the possible western railroad routes from Wisconsin and Illinois. The forming of territorial government in Kansas-Nebraska would allow the federal government to allot land grants along a potential rail route to the company building the railroad. In a land-rich and capital-poor country, this was the way to provide public financing for a vital infrastructure improvement—and feather his own nest.

A second motivation stems from a similar source. As the leader of the West, Douglas knew westerners' hunger for land for farming, ranching, and mining and the vital speculation in land that went with them. Territorial government would open that vast swath of territory to settlement, development, and, eventually, incorporation into the Union. Douglas dreamed of a vast West that would be the pivot wheel around which the nation would turn. To fulfill his ambition for the presidency and the interests of his section, he needed to open western territory. The lure of a route to the now-populous state of California and the ports to the Pacific beyond was too great a temptation to ignore.

Douglas was not alone in his dreams of westward expansion. The so-called F Street Mess, because they ate and resided in the same boardinghouse on F Street in Washington, D.C., of Andrew P. Butler from South Carolina, James M. Mason and Robert M. T. Hunter from Virginia, and David R. Atchison from Missouri were all heirs of Calhoun and extremely sympathetic to western Missouri's slaveholders, who wanted to cross the Missouri River into the Kansas-Nebraska Territory with their slaves. They were committed to slavery's expansion, and the existence of slavery on the eastern bank of the Missouri attested to its sustainability on the western bank. Furthermore, they felt that the South needed another slave state to offset the nominally free state of California, despite California's Democratic senators' adherence to the South. Last, and certainly not least, they were unhappy with the Missouri Compromise line as both a matter of principle—prohibitions on slavery being anathema—and part of their psychology. The Missouri Compromise had been a defeat for their cause. In their present mood, they felt that they were on the defensive against the free-soil movement, for it and abolitionism had become inextricably intertwined in their minds.

It is also possible that Douglas and the F Street Mess may have been collaborating on a project to rescue the Democratic Party from the Pierce administration's fumbling party politics. Even though the now-dominant Hunkers were in control of New York, Pierce insisted on awarding some patronage appointments to the remaining Barnburners and the Hunkers who favored reconciliation between the two camps—the Softshell Hunkers. The Hunkers opposed to reconciliation—the Hardshells—objected to Pierce's largesse to their enemies. As a result of these squabbles, the Whigs had an opening to recover from their losses in 1852. A test of party loyalty, such as votes on popular sovereignty in Kansas-Nebraska, would clear out the malingerers from the Democratic ranks and damage the Whigs by reraising the issue of expansion, their weakness ever since the Texas annexation controversy.

Whatever Douglas's intentions might have been, he proceeded with his plan to disastrous result. The recently quieted dispute over the expansion of slavery flared up again with a vengeance. His first version of a Kansas-Nebraska Act, on January 4, tried to sidestep the issue of popular sovereignty by noting that the Compromise of 1850 had made it law with the Utah and New Mexico Territories' legislation. This did not satisfy the F Street Mess. Douglas responded by adding a section to the bill proclaiming that there had been an error in the printing. Even this language did not satisfy his messmates. By January 24 he produced a version that appeased Atchison and other southern Democrats. Douglas now began his greatest challenge as a legislative leader.

Whereas the outcome of the Kansas-Nebraska bill could not be in doubt—after all Democrats had solid majorities in both Houses and President Pierce was behind it—Douglas must have been surprised at the vehemence it spurred among its northern opponents. Up to the time when the House finally gave its consent in May, speeches, demonstrations, newspaper broadsides, and fierce debates raged in the North. On the defensive because of their party's official statement that the Compromise of 1850 was the final word on slavery extension—only Conscience Whigs such as New York Senator William H. Seward had opposed the Compromise of 1850—Whigs were vulnerable to the challenge of Free-Soilers such as Ohio Senator Salmon P. Chase and Representative Joshua Giddings, as well as Charles Sumner, who could reject the Kansas-Nebraska bill outright. Joined by Missouri's Thomas Hart Benton, they extolled the virtues of the Missouri Compromise line. Radicals such as Seward and Sumner went further, to denounce the ploy of the "slave power" to regain its control of federal policy.

Sumner Speaks

On February 21, 1854, Sumner delivered an oration entitled "The Landmark of Freedom" to rebut Douglas's opening defense of the bill. Like all of Sumner's speeches, it was written out in detail over the preceding days. He then memorized all several thousand words of it. A combination of legal brief and public discourse, it laid out why the Kansas-Nebraska bill was contrary to both law and the nation's original understandings of the limits of slavery. Particularly galling to senators such as Andrew P. Butler was Sumner's claim that the South's politicians were breaking the promise they made in 1820: "With the consideration in its pocket, it [the South] repudiates the bargain which it forced upon the country."[4] The word "consideration" is a legal term for use in determining whether or not a promise is a contract. Sumner, the lawyer, was informing his fellow attorneys that the South was in breach. He was also issuing a kind of challenge. A man of honor did not break his word— for his word was a public statement, and going back on it brought shame.

Butler, besides being a lawyer, had served for several decades as a state judge. His colleagues often referred to him using that title. He well knew what "consideration" was and what Sumner was alleging. There may be some doubt, however, that Sumner, who had never been to the South, fully understood the severity of such a charge to a gentleman of honor. To be viewed as breaking one's word was a dishonor of the severest character. This was outside of the normal accusations of politics. Sumner had impugned their reputations, their most valuable asset. The miscommunication, or perhaps the simple gap between the two sections' notions of breach, would lead to an escalation of accusations. In any case, Butler's rebuke of Sumner for an insult Sumner did not intend would be severe.

Drawing on the substantial jurisprudence of the antislavery movement, Sumner also assailed the doctrine of popular sovereignty. Once again his arguments were both legal and political. First, he asserted that the Constitution of 1787 was based on freedom, not slavery. Second, he posited that the common law, which the United States inherited from England, was antislavery. Last, and certainly not least, he repeated Seward's notion that natural law had no place for human bondage. Therefore, "beyond the sphere of these [local municipal] laws, it ceases to exist," with the exception of the Fugitive Slave Law.[5] These arguments were the same as those of other abolitionist advocates. For example, Lysander Spooner wrote in his *The Unconstitutional-*

ity of Slavery, "constitutional law, under any form of government, consists of only those principles of the written constitution that are consistent with natural law, and man's natural rights."[6] Here was the great fear of the South. Although the Fifth Amendment might guarantee their slave property when taken from a slave state into another jurisdiction, it did not protect the property interest in the offspring or allow for the forcible coercion and slave codes that protected slavery as an institution.

Butler responded harshly to Sumner's idealistic arguments. In taking his rhetoric to another level, Butler set the stage for later events. Instead of merely defending his section against Sumner's assertions, Butler decided to lambaste northern society and morals and decry the "cankers" of its society— the temperance movement, abolitionism, and women "who step from the sphere proscribed to them by God, to enter into the political arena, and claim the rights of men."[7] It was one thing to defend slavery. It was another to call into question the values of the people of another section and Massachusetts in particular. Perhaps inadvertently, Sumner had succeeded in goading Butler into a sectional attack, rather than a mere defense.

On March 3, Douglas sparred with Sumner, but with sharper and more personal words than Butler. Douglas sneered at the difficulty Sumner had gaining election to the Senate and likened the coalition of Democrats and Free-Soilers that made it happen as akin to a "larceny." Sumner had come to the Senate, according to Douglas, through "dishonorable and corrupt means."[8] It was not the first time a senator had replied to Sumner's legal arguments with an ad hominem attack. Douglas accused Sumner, along with Ohio's Salmon Chase, of being "the pure, unadulterated representatives of Abolitionism, Free Soilism, Niggerism in the Congress of the United States."[9]

On the one hand, had Sumner hailed from South Carolina, he might well have felt honor bound to avenge these insults with a cane or a pistol. Certainly they were meant to shame him as a man undeserving of the title and status of a respectable gentleman worthy of a duel. On the other hand, one tried-and-true abolitionist tactic was to try to goad slavery's defenders into excesses of personal vituperation. Sumner could hardly have expected to win allies by his belligerent oratory. However, this mistakenly assumes that Sumner was trying to forge legislative coalitions. Sumner was speaking to an audience beyond the Senate chamber. In other words, he was using the Senate chamber as an amplification device so that he could draw attention to his cause.

He pursued the same objective in his speech on May 25 after the House and Senate had passed the Kansas-Nebraska Act. This time he presented some additional signatures to a petition Harriet Beecher Stowe had financed from the profits of her book, *Uncle Tom's Cabin*. Rather than uphold the wall of separation between church and state, Sumner gloried in the role ministers played in the founding and governance of colonial New England and the implications of New England's ministers condemning slavery extension as they had supported the American Revolution. "In a Christian land, and in an age of civilization, a time-honored statute of Freedom [the Missouri Compromise] is struck down, opening the way to all the countless woes and wrongs of human bondage."[10] This religious language was both a rhetorical device and a substantive point. Sumner wanted to make it plain that religious justifications for slavery were more than just wrong; they were immoral in and of themselves. Mason objected to the petition in no uncertain terms. He viewed it as an "unholy alliance" between ministers and a political party.[11] Ministers in the South had long since become staunch defenders of slavery.

As charged as these exchanges were, events in Massachusetts caused an intensification of feeling. Pursuant to the Fugitive Slave Law, an accused runaway slave named Anthony Burns was held in the Boston courthouse awaiting extradition to Virginia. On May 26, 1854, the day after Sumner told the Senate that violent resistance to the law was inevitable, a crowd accosted the men that the federal marshal had hired to help guard the putative fugitive. In the scuffle that followed, one of the men died from a gunshot wound. Echoing the sentiments of many Southerners, *The Washington Evening Star* placed the blame on Sumner even though Boston had not received word of Sumner's speech until after the incident. As if their implicit threat against him was not alarming enough, Sumner decided to make a speech in the Senate supporting a petition from Massachusetts for repeal of the Fugitive Slave Law on June 26, 1854.

In the course of these remarks, Sumner declared that opposition to the Fugitive Slave Law was the same as opposition to the Stamp Act in 1765. He defended the Bostonians' actions against Tennessee Senator James C. Jones's accusation that it was treason to oppose federal law with the declaration, "Her traitors now are those who are truly animated by the spirit of the American Revolution."[12] Butler was unwilling to let this assertion go uncontested. He reminded Sumner that not only was Massachusetts a slaveholding state at the time, but its representatives had entered into a compact with the South.

The ironies in this exchange abound, particularly in light of later events. Sumner was defending lawlessness in the name of a higher law of human freedom, comparing the Burns mob to the anti–Stamp Act demonstrators of 1765. In the winter of 1860–61, South Carolina secessionists would be comparing themselves to the revolutionaries of 1776 and declaring that their lawlessness was dictated by individual rights to self-government and private property.

At one point in the exchange, Butler decided to interrogate Sumner on whether he would enforce the law of the land. This was a breach of etiquette. One always addressed the chair of the Senate, not individual members. Nevertheless, Sumner replied, "Does the honorable Senator ask me if I would personally join in sending a fellow-man into bondage? 'Is thy servant a dog, that he should do this thing?'"[13] Not pleased with either the quotation from scripture or the sentiment it expressed, Butler mocked Sumner for his literary bent.

Mason went further. Like Butler and Maryland's former governor Thomas G. Pratt, Mason became incensed with Sumner's reply that he would not uphold the Fugitive Slave Law and his characterization of Burns's owner as a "slave-catcher." Apparently slave traders and slave trackers, including the class of men who pursued runaway slaves, were not equal in dignity (in southern eyes) to the men who owned the slaves and did business with the traders and trackers. "I say, sir, the dignity of the American Senate has been rudely, wantonly, grossly assailed by a Senator from Massachusetts, and not only the dignity of the Senate, but of the whole people." If these heated declarations were not enough, Mason added, "Why, sir, am I speaking of a fanatic, one whose reason is dethroned!"[14] It is hard to understand why Mason and Butler would be so upset over Sumner's reply. After all, his oath as a senator was not to faithfully execute the law, but to uphold and be loyal.

Sumner had become the lightening rod for southern proslavery fury. Two days later, Alabama's Clement C. Clay delivered another assault on Sumner. He proclaimed that Sumner not only was committing "moral perjury" by his refusal to render alleged slaves to their supposed masters but was dishonestly attempting to change the *Congressional Globe* to alter the record of what he had said. What was Clay's suggested punishment for such crimes? He prescribed that Sumner should be shunned "like a leper, and loathed like a filthy reptile."[15] Such a treatment and the labels to go with them were quite harsh even for the oratory and politics of the 1850s Senate. Compared to these remarks, Sumner's comments on Douglas, Mason, and Butler two years later were milk-and-water things, neither novel nor particularly vicious.

It was true that Sumner advocated passionately, heaping calumniation on his opponents. But one should note that all of these remarks were part of prepared orations. While not the conciliatory high tones of a Daniel Webster or a Henry Clay, nor the generalized fustian of a John C. Calhoun, they were the zealous advocacy of a religious-minded lawyer on behalf of abolition. By making himself into a target, Sumner drew on another tradition, less rhetorical and more personal, among reformers.

Sumner drew on Henry David Thoreau's ideal of nonviolent resistance. Thoreau allowed himself to be hauled off to jail rather than pay taxes to support an immoral war in Mexico. As Thoreau wrote in "Resistance to Civil Government" (1849), an essay that Sumner read, "Can there not be a government in which the majorities do not virtually decide right and wrong, but conscience? . . . The only obligation which I have a right to assume is to do at any time what I think right . . . I cannot for an instant recognize that political organization as my government which is the slave's government also . . . What I have to do is to see, at any rate, that I do not lend myself to the wrong which I condemn." It might seem odd for a senator, an insider, to adopt Thoreau's pose of moral prophet, the essential outsider, but that is just what Sumner did. He took upon himself the calumny of the slaveholders because to compromise or to avert his eyes from the evil was to condone it. Thoreau again: "A very few—as heroes, patriots, martyrs, reformers in the great sense, and men—serve the state with their consciences." In later years, Mohandas K. Gandhi would deploy passive resistance in India to resist the British Raj. Martin Luther King Jr., in the American South in the second half of the twentieth century, would embrace the same tactics to great effect. Sumner was using his determination, his words, and his moral purity to provoke a response from his opponents. Only in this way could he hope to motivate the latent, largely pro-compromise North into righteous anger against the "slave power."

Sumner proffered his own answer as to why Butler, Clay, and Mason were so vehemently opposed to him and his speeches that same day, June 28, 1854. Quoting from none other than Thomas Jefferson, he believed the source of the acrimony to come from the nature of slavery itself. As for his answer to Butler on his oath to uphold the Constitution, he quoted from Andrew Jackson's message on the Bank of the United States veto. Per the reasoning of one of the founders of the Democratic Party, Sumner was obligated only to uphold the Constitution as "I understand it." Further, he reminded his audience that South Carolina herself had passed laws interfering with the federal mails to remove any abolitionist literature and forced the expulsion of Samuel Hoar from the state for disturbing the peace.[16] Hoar had come to Charleston to inquire about the imprisonment of a Massachusetts black sailor. Interestingly, the gentleman to whom the governor of South Carolina had entrusted this escort duty was none other than Preston S. Brooks.

Sumner was not finished. As Mason and Butler had aimed their venom at Massachusetts, so Sumner turned to South Carolina. Developing two issues he would raise in his "Crime against Kansas" speech, he expounded on South Carolina's contribution to the Revolution and the personal characteristics of Butler, that state's great defender. Earlier Sumner mentioned that Butler's speech "gurgles forth."[17] This was likely a veiled reference to the fact that Butler had developed a speech impediment, possibly from a mild stroke. If that were not enough, Sumner went on to counter Butler's argument that both slaveholding Massachusetts and South Carolina had made the Revolution. Citing published histories and the remarks of one of South Carolina's first representatives to Congress, he showed that the South and South Carolina in particular had not contributed nearly as many troops to the cause as the North because slavery required that they withhold many to police their black population.

Butler did not allow Sumner the last word. Rejecting a call for adjournment, he tried to rebut Sumner's history. Primarily he relied on the construction of the word "slaveholding." He rejected Sumner's definition for his own: if there were slaves in a state, it was slaveholding. While most scholars today would support Sumner's definition, which mandated that slavery be a foundational institution of the society rather than an incidental one, Butler was not concerned with such niceties. He pronounced Sumner's speech a "libel." Anyone with knowledge of the law knew that this meant a deliberate falsification damaging to the other party. In effect, Butler was calling Sumner a liar. Finally, he put his own cast on the events of the American Revolution. Boston and Massachusetts had started the conflict and South Carolina came to their aid. "Upon false issues he has made the speech," Butler concluded.[18] Like other Southerners defending slavery, Butler had to rewrite his state's history in order to reconcile it with the "peculiar institution."

Again, why were Butler, Mason, and Clay, among others, so upset at Sumner that they purposefully accused him of the worst character flaws and illegal, possibly treasonous behavior? After all, Sumner had no battalions—he was not the leader of a faction in the Senate or any party in general. We must return to this question because it shows that the "Crime against Kansas" speech was not an isolated event. The escalation began far earlier. Sumner's rhetorical flourishes were met with excited refutations and countercharges that exceeded the usual thrust and parrying of Senate debate. Certainly, there was the tenor of the time. The Kansas-Nebraska Act debates had reopened the old feelings of sectional strife. In the House, debate became so heated that Henry A. Edmundson, Brooks's friend, pulled pistols and aimed them at Lewis D. Campbell of Ohio. Only after the sergeant at arms took Edmundson into custody was order restored to the floor. Then again, there was also the pervasive fear among Southerners that northern resistance to the laws necessary to slavery's preservation, like the Fugitive Slave Law, would be enough to undo slavery everywhere, not just in the territories.

With the bad taste from these exchanges lingering in their mouths, all sides went back to their respective homes to campaign. The contest over Kansas-Nebraska spurred two important developments. One was the formation of a new party in the Upper Midwest, the Republican Party, dedicated to opposing the extension of slavery in the territories. Over the course of the next two years, Conscience Whigs such as Seward would join it, along with Free-Soilers such as Chase and Sumner. Indeed, in the radical wing of the Republican Party Sumner found his true political home. Unfortunately for the new party, at first they would have to fight not only the remaining Whigs and the Democrats but the meteoric rise of another force: the American Party.

The American Party owed its formation to nativist, anti-immigrant, anti-Catholic secret societies like New York City's Order of the Star Spangled Banner. It received its nickname, the "Know-Nothings," from its members' preset response when asked about their organization, "I know nothing." At the peak of their influence between 1854 and 1856, they had over a million members, elected a majority of the Massachusetts legislature, and were decisive forces in the election of Chicago's and San Francisco's mayors, as well as the governor of California. In their campaign platform for 1856, during which they nominated Millard Fillmore for president, they called for a twenty-one-year wait for immigrants to become citizens, only Protestant teachers in the public schools, Bible readings in all classrooms, restrictions on immigration from Catholic countries, barring foreign-born immigrants from public office, and prohibition of alcohol. Their violent, bullying tactics eventually alienated the public but were instrumental in the destruction of the Whig Party in the North and South.

The election of 1854 prefigured the end of the Second Party System—where Democrats squared off against Whigs in both the North and South—with the Democrats unified behind popular sovereignty and the North divided among Democrats, the newly formed Republican Party, and the Know-Nothings. The remnant of the Whig Party was caught between the Republicans and Know-Nothings in the North and between the Democrats and Know-Nothings in the South. As a result, the Whig Party disappeared as a national force. An alliance between Republicans and the Know-Nothings would make them the majority party in the Electoral College as a result of the predominance of the free states' population, an alliance that would come in 1856. Correspondingly, the gutting of Democratic support in the North made that party even more beholden to the slave South.

The Pierce administration's southern sympathies became a critical problem when Kansas politics proved popular sovereignty to be critically flawed. Because the Kansas-Nebraska Act did not specify what it took to be a resident of the territory for the purpose of electing the legislature, proslavery Missourians crossed the river into Kansas to make the legislature their own. On occasion these Missourians, whom Horace Greeley called "border ruffians," actually did stuff ballot boxes, as on Election Day in Kansas, March 30, 1855. In one round of voting, although there were only twenty-nine hundred registered voters, over six thousand ballots were cast. When the result was announced, a proslavery legislature was the victor of an obvious fraud. The proslavery legislature then wrote a series of slave laws for the territory. In protest, the free-state legislators walked out and formed their own legislature in Topeka. In a message to Congress in January 1856, Franklin Pierce, siding with proslavery forces, declared the Topeka government to be a "revolution" against the lawful government. With members of the New England Emigrant Aid Company heeding Reverend Henry Ward Beecher's call for money to send rifles to Kansas, the stage was set for violent confrontation. Oddly enough, the nation would only learn of the border ruffians' "Sack of Lawrence," a gang assault by proslavery forces on an antislavery town (in which the only fatality was the death of a ruffian from the collapse of a hotel), after Brooks had caned Sumner.

On May 19 and 20, Charles Sumner gave his much-anticipated "Crime against Kansas" speech. Spectators packed the galleries, and the Senate floor filled with his colleagues. The South's delegation continued to follow Clay's policy of shunning the Bay State's senior senator. Sumner was not motivated solely by his antislavery animus. Events in Massachusetts caused him great concern. The Know-Nothing governor, Henry J. Gardner, was openly maneuvering for the legislature to put him in place of Sumner in the Senate. The coalition of 1851 was long gone. Once again, Sumner's lack of accomplishment in the Senate worked against him, as did his penchant for making enemies and alienating would-be allies. He was convinced that he needed a splendid oration to save his faltering fortunes back home.

The occasion for his address was Douglas's attempt, on behalf of the Pierce administration, to recognize Kansas's proslavery government. Douglas blamed the disorder in Kansas on the abolitionists who, abetted by emigrant aid societies, were in rebellion against the natural settlers of Kansas, the Missourians. Seward opposed him and moved for the admission of Kansas as a free state under the Topeka Constitution. In between these two poles was the complicated truth that Kansas was suffering the usual turmoil of a recently settled frontier territory. Violence was largely personal, as much about land titles, office-holding, and the location of towns as it was about the presence of slavery. For Sumner, however, with the letters from his antislavery correspondents in hand, the issues were plain as day.

As was his practice, Sumner prepared his massive speech over the preceding two weeks. By the time he delivered the first part on May 19, he had committed it to memory. All of the pointed remarks about Mason, Douglas, and Butler had been crafted, honed to a razor-sharp edge, and embedded into the lyrical stanzas. Many commentators then and thereafter have criticized Sumner for abusing Butler, then absent from the chamber. But Sumner likely did not plan for Butler's sudden absence. Even so, it did not matter. For Sumner, the die was cast.

The speech was divided into many parts: the "crime" committed against Kansas by the "slave power," the "apologies" for the crime—in other words, Douglas's presentation—and the redress for the crime. Sumner began with an attack on Butler and Douglas, although not by name. He compared them to Don Quixote and Sancho Panza, the tall, elderly aristocrat who insanely believed he was a knight of old and his short, paunchy would-be squire from the Spanish classic novel *Don Quixote*, by Miguel de Cervantes Saavedra. Given their respective physical forms, it was an apt and mocking allusion. Sumner described Butler's advocacy for slavery in vivid terms, language quoted in all the accounts of this speech: "Of course he has chosen a mistress to whom he has made his vows, and who, though ugly to others, is always lovely to him; though polluted in the sight of the world, is chaste in his sight—I mean the harlot Slavery."[19] In this well-researched, formal style, Sumner lambasted his opponents.

It is also important to note the sexual imagery that recurred throughout the oration, which was neither accidental nor without precedent. Abolitionists routinely accused slaveholders of maintaining slavery so that they could engage in forcible sexual relations with their slaves. In 1858, Wendell Phillips went so far as to call the South a gigantic brothel in a speech in Boston. If Brooks was telling the truth about being in the audience on the first day, he could not mistake Sumner's accusation: "It is the rape of a virgin Territory, compelling it to the hateful embrace of Slavery; and it may be clearly traced to a depraved longing for a new slave State, the hideous offspring of such a crime, in the hope of adding to the power of Slavery in the national Government."[20] Southerners were depraved, lascivious, and beastly, the exact opposite of their self-image under the honor code. Like other abolitionists before him, Sumner turned racial animus on its head. Southerners did not practice slavery because African-Americans were disgusting beasts, but because Southerners found them sexually appealing.

The bulk of the second part of this two-day presentation was Sumner's version of the events in Kansas. To summarize: proslavery forces under Missourians such as former Senator Atchison, with the connivance of the Pierce administration, forced a proslavery government on the territory using force of arms, conspiracy, and voting illegalities. The "*causing cause*" was the desire to perpetuate the slave power's hold over the national government by adding another slave state to the Union, breaking the South's agreement with the North in the Missouri Compromise.[21] To buttress his arguments, he quoted from letters, official papers, and on-the-ground testimony.

In the third part of the speech, Sumner attempted to debunk the arguments that others, mostly Douglas, used to justify the admission of Kansas under its proslavery government. He labeled these apologies the "tyrannical," the "imbecile," the "absurd," and the "infamous."[22] The first label he applied to the actions of the ruffians, the second to the Pierce administration's protests that it could do nothing to police the elections, the third to the idea that Kansas's territorial government could allow for slavery, and the fourth to Douglas's attack on the New England Emigrant Aid Society as a violent, illegal, abolitionist conspiracy. He stressed facts, offered classical allusions, and made legal points that drew on his earlier pronouncements that the U.S. Constitution, the founding fathers, and natural law were all hostile to slavery's expansion.

In the fourth part of the oration, Sumner traversed the four remedies before the Senate in the following form: "the remedy of Tyranny; next the remedy of Folly; next, the Remedy of Injustice and Civil War; and fourthly, the Remedy of Justice and Peace."[23] The first three were those of his opponents, the last was Seward's counterproposal, that Kansas be admitted as a free state. Sumner cited precedent; historical analogies, including the circumstances of the American Revolution; the writings of Andrew Jackson; St. George Tucker on Blackstone; and poetry to support his arguments. Almost all the way through this exposition there was very little to find objectionable. Passionate, biting, and occasionally mocking, Sumner had not gone beyond anything one might find in college classes on rhetoric.

However, he did not stop his lengthy address there. Sumner continued to compare Kansas and her situation to that of the colonies and the circumstances that brought the American Revolution. On this foundation he built an attack on Butler, South Carolina, and Douglas. One may surmise that he felt that he was owed some payback. In any case, mocking the still-absent senator's physical problems, Sumner referred to both the "loose expectoration of his speech" and the untruthfulness of his arguments: "But the senator touches nothing that he does not disfigure—with error, sometimes of principle, sometimes of fact." Comparing South Carolina with Kansas, he opined, "Were the whole history of South Carolina blotted out of existence . . . civilization might lose—I do not say how little; but surely less than it has already gained by the example of Kansas."[24] Sumner employed the rhetorical device of exaggeration for the purpose of emphasis. Sumner's larger point was not that Butler and South Carolina required calumniation, but that Kansas, by fighting against slavery, was deserving of praise. Still, if one only wanted to hear the few words of mockery, they were certainly there.

After again assailing Douglas, Sumner mentioned Mason, whom he accused of betraying the legacy of Washington and Jefferson's Virginia. Then, in his closing, he made his purpose clear. He was not attempting to persuade his colleagues. He was making an appeal to the nation in anticipation of the election of 1856. "To the People, now on the eve of exercising the electoral

franchise, in choosing a Chief Magistrate of the Republic, I appeal, to vindi-
cate the electoral franchise in Kansas."[25] He placed his trust in history and
God, not in a Senate majority. As Thoreau had written, "a government in
which the majority rule in all cases can not be based on justice, even as far
as men understand it." There was, after all, a great religious conviction in his
abolitionism.

Now one can view the incendiary remarks about Butler and South Carolina in their proper context, within the whole of the speech, and Sumner's
overarching purpose. He had delivered an elaborate oration filled with classical quotations, legal references, and rhetorical devices meant for a national
audience. As the poet and abolitionist John Greenleaf Whittier wrote, it was
"a grand and terrible philippic, worthy of the great occasion; the severe and
awful truth which the sharp agony of the national crisis demanded."[26] Accustomed to attacking Sumner on every occasion, his opponents leapt on the
few personal allusions with the fierceness of tigers.

It was not surprising that several of his fellow senators denounced the
oration. Even Sumner's friend and ally Seward worried that the personal de-
nunciations were gratuitous. Unfortunately, we cannot credit their public
criticisms. Sumner's enemies would not have pronounced on the speech and
the speaker unless they had formulated the remarks for public view. In other
words, they saw in Sumner's public appeal the opportunity to appeal to their
own electorates. If Sumner's comments had to be wrenched out of context,
they happily applied themselves to the task. Douglas's oft-quoted remark may
be more telling as it seems to have been impromptu: "Is it his object to provoke some of us to kick him as we would a dog in the street, that he may
get sympathy upon the just chastisement?" Just as memorable, but certainly
not as accurate, was Lewis Cass's description of the speech as "the most un-
American and unpatriotic that ever grated on the ears of the members of this
high body."[27]

In this fashion, the so-called machine that would go of itself produced
a deep, fractious, and vituperative divide between the defenders and expo-
nents of slavery and their opponents. If it were an impersonal mechanism, it
was hurtling the nation toward violent conflict. But, as the foregoing history
makes plain, it was not a machine that would go of itself. Very real people
made a great many decisions that brought the nation to the point where one
congressman would attack another. If anything, it was more like a waltz, with

all the partners moving in time to the music. The couples might change, but the movements were eerily the same.

One may say that all but one of Sumner's critics took his remarks in stride. They used words to combat words. One critic reacted differently. Brooks later testified that he was in the chamber to hear Sumner make his remarks regarding Butler and the invidious comparison between Kansas and South Carolina. The question is, does his oft-repeated protestation that Sumner had impugned the honor of a "friend and relative" and his native state actually reflect his motivation for his assault?[28] The answer lies in a close examination of his official statements, his private letters, the environs both he and Sumner inhabited, and the aftermath of what Brooks made no apology for doing two days after Sumner completed his lengthy brief to the nation.

3 } IMMEDIATE AFTERMATH

AFTER THE assault on May 22, 1856, the protagonists were tried in several forums at the same time: before the Congress, in the court of public opinion, and, in Brooks's case alone, in criminal court. The verdict depended on the forum. Different rules applied in each, but regardless of the differences, the response of each has much to tell us not only about the incident itself but also about the nature of the Congress, the public, and the criminal courts. The United States was in the midst of a tremendous transition in all of these realms. How they dealt with this incident indicates something of the nature of that transformation.

Brooks and His City

The Congress's consideration of the incident took place in Washington, D.C., the very setting of the caning. It was not a particularly favorable venue for Sumner or his friends and allies. The nation's capital was a southern city and intentionally so. Its location on the Potomac between Maryland and Virginia was Alexander Hamilton's concession to the South so he could receive southern support for his financial policies. Despite George Washington's and John Adams's plans for a grand, imposing capital with broad avenues, public monuments, and impressive buildings, it was more like an unfinished project.

Southern ladies and matrons dominated high society with their salons, balls, and parties. The hotels, boardinghouses, and public spaces were populated with slaves, southern cuisine, and southern amusements. The climate was that of the lower Chesapeake. Hot and humid in summer, light winters, and pestilential from the refuse dumped into its streets and the effluvial wastes draining, on its better days, into the canal, Washington, D.C.'s only notable landmarks were the Capitol Building, then under construction for the transformation into the expansive edifice we know today, and the half-finished Washington Monument. The streets were made of dirt that became mud in rain and the source of dust storms in dry weather. Congressmen who could not afford houses in the fashionable district lodged in boardinghouses. One could find culture and high society alongside slave auctions and slums. Crime became such a serious problem during the 1850s that Congress conducted a special investigation.

They did not have to look far to find the true source of the city's many ills. It was Congress, itself. A federal government of limited powers had to have a capital that reflected its inferior status. A truly magnificent capital with all the amenities, services, and facilities of a modern city would have been the commitment of a different nation. It did not have that nation, at least not yet.

There was one aspect of capital life that worked well: news spread fast. For the next few weeks following the assault, the city was afire with the dispute over the matter. Senators and representatives filled the *Congressional Globe* with their views of the incident, reviews of the speech that preceded it, and everything in between. Representatives from Massachusetts and South Carolina spent time defending their respective states and assaulting their opposites'. Senators lined up to alternately accuse Brooks of barbarism and make a martyr of Sumner or to place the blame for the assault squarely on Sumner and praise Brooks for his defense of his relative and his state. Butler returned from the sickbed of his son to come to the rescue of his cousin's son, Brooks.

But what was Brooks's motive and character? All we have of Preston S. Brooks's reasons for assaulting Sumner are his own words for either public or private consumption, and they contradict one another in important ways. His carefully, modestly framed testimony before the House investigating committee, his public speeches, and his statement before a criminal judge in Washington, D.C., all contrast with the braggadocio of his private correspondence. What is more, his death soon thereafter gave a luster to his life and statements only a premature passing can imbue. The reverberations of the tributes in the House and Senate, in newspapers, and at the monument at his grave site lasted all the way into the twentieth century, when scholars looked anew at the attack. Colored by their view of the Civil War that followed, many historians have chosen to portray Brooks as a moderate aroused by an uncivil attack partly because it better fits the idea that the nation's politicians stumbled into war, rather than assigning blame to one section of the country.

Although Brooks may have gained his first term in Congress as the result of siding with a more moderate faction in South Carolina, his speeches suggest that this might have been more the result of a family-related rivalry with the faction Wigfall supported than any moderate or nationalist sentiment. In fact, in his first major speech in Congress on March 15, 1854, on the Kansas-Nebraska bill, he stated, "Sir, there is a suspicious sound in that word *national*, which jars upon southern ears, and when coupled with the doctrines it inculcates, comes athwart the gale like the low whistle of the bandit, and admonishes honest men to look well to the security of their estates." By implication dishonest and corrupt men were nationalists. He also made clear his defense of the South and slavery in the proven profitability of the cash crops, as well as "the fact, that the elevation and Christianization of the negro is only to be effected by his servitude to a superior race, and the ameliorating influence of an intelligence borrowed from the white man."[1] For Brooks, racism and economic interest happily coincided.

That he was in truth a servant of his section he demonstrated in his second major speech in Congress on the Pacific railroad—also known as the transcontinental railroad—on June 14, 1854. He opposed it. This was despite his professed friendship for his fellow Democrats in California. He offered two reasons for his objection. First, under his states' rights view of the Constitution, the federal government did not have the authority to contravene the individual states' grant of the lands, which were proposed for a northern route, to the federal government. "The Government is not a proprietor, but a trustee, holding lands for the States which created it." Second, he wanted the route to be a southern one because it alone would come from the Mexican Cession and would be privately financed. To answer the claim that he was being a sectionalist, he professed a change in his attitude: "The time has been when I was sectional, and it has passed." He had replaced it with a different word "which is more elevated and patriotic, the word *constitutional*."[2]

In the famous words of Supreme Court Justice Oliver Wendell Holmes Jr., this is "a distinction without a difference." That Brooks (unlike the fire-eaters) did not threaten secession if the demands of the South were not met was not an endorsement of a "nationalist" point of view; it was only the confidence of the member of a party and section that were now in control of the national government. He could afford such non-concessions. The benefits of a southern route for the railroad would naturally accrue to the South. It was not just an aid to southern production; it would orient the Mexican Cession's territories and future states to the South just as the river transportation leading to New Orleans had fastened ties among the southern Midwest, Kentucky, Tennessee, and the rest of the old Southwest to the Southeast.

It was in that spirit that he offered his resolutions on the bearing of firearms into the House on June 21, 1854, a piece of evidence several scholars have used to show his abhorrence of violence. The first of these would have provided for expulsion by a two-thirds vote of any member bringing a deadly weapon into the chamber. The second would have had the members stow them in a rack outside the chamber for public view. When viewed in context of the dispute that had broken out in the House on the Kansas-Nebraska bill in the preceding days, his remarks were not so much pacific in origin, but rather jocular and concerned with honor: "The first of the resolutions I presented is founded in propriety, in honor, and in wisdom, and I shall insist upon its being added to the rules of the House. The other was intended to ridicule an unmanly and pernicious habit, and to restore by a jest the harmony of the House, which was fast becoming excited and divided."[3] Brooks was not opposed to the violent settlement of a dispute; he was concerned that such settlements should not appear unseemly.

On another occasion, on December 24, 1855, he made a statement that his defenders and eulogizers attributed to his moderate stance on the issues: "I have been taunted at home with being a little too national," he asserted in the course of the prolonged debate on who should be Speaker of the House. "My patriotism and my duty to my fellow-men compel me to do all that I can to preserve this Government, so long as it is administered according to the intent and meaning of the Constitution."[4] Despite its surface moderation, this assertion actually restated his advocacy of the states' rights position over any other interpretation that would allow for limits on slavery's expansion. Similarly, his endorsement of the Republicans' Nathaniel P. Banks or Joshua Giddings for Speaker over the Southerner, William R. Smith from Alabama, was because he wanted to denounce Smith's membership in and endorsement of the anti-Catholic and immigrant American Party.[5] Brooks was not seriously favoring Republicans out of national sentiment, but to lay claim to his true convictions as a Democrat. Brooks's "nationalism" was his sectionalism and partisanship by another name.

If Brooks actually felt that his chastisement of Sumner would be received in much the same way as his speeches, he was sorely mistaken. More likely than not, Brooks himself was not doing a lot of thinking once he determined to punish Sumner. His culture extolled the manly and hid deep-set class anxieties. His personal psychology reinforced this mind-set. Losing his brother, his father's favorite, in a war he himself had largely missed played a role in his desire to be seen as an exemplar of valorous self-help. His own sense of what was right and just was fixed in this constellation of personal needs and fears, just as Sumner's need to be in the antislavery vanguard reflected his own sense of inadequacy.

Brooks freely admitted his own powerlessness to force Sumner to conform to southern customs. Sumner, as a Northerner, would not have accepted a duel. At the same time, Brooks also confessed that "the Senator was my superior in strength."[6] Brooks did not act as a challenger with confidence, but one riddled with concerns about the legal ramifications, his opponent's character, and his own vulnerability. In some ways, he epitomized the South during the 1850s. Feeling overwhelmed and under assault from a superior rival, he sought both revenge and dominance.

As for the proposition that South Carolinians were under siege from all of Washington, D.C., after Sumner's "Crime against Kansas" aspersions, this would have been a powerful motivator if true. It was not. The Pulitzer Prize–winning biography of Charles Sumner's life before the Civil War would have us believe otherwise: "Though no attacks were made upon him on May 20, Southerners were still angrily discussing his speech. A South Carolinian, it was said, 'could not go into a parlor, or drawing-room, or to a dinner party, where he did not find an implied reproach that there was unmanly submission to an insult to his State and his countrymen.'"[7] However, the source was not a neutral observer. The comment was Andrew Butler's defense of Brooks on June 13, 1856, after Butler had returned to Washington, D.C. Butler attempted to quiet the blowback, during which the House was moving to expel Brooks and Keitt for their behavior.[8] It was an excuse after the fact made by Brooks's de facto defense attorney on the floor of the Senate.

The more likely situation was that Brooks, Keitt, and Edmundson from Virginia were simply sharing the community's condemnation of Sumner's speech. After all, as Brooks himself stated earlier in the session on December

24, 1855: "We are standing upon slave territory, surrounded by slave States, and pride, honor, patriotism, all command us, if a battle is to be fought, to fight it here upon this floor."[9] While the drawing rooms of Washington, D.C., were likely filled with condemnation of Sumner and the arguments of an honor culture, South Carolinians were applying the reproach to themselves, not the other way around. We must also remember that Brooks spent two days with Keitt fortifying himself and, more likely than not, receiving a great deal of encouragement from his hot-tempered friend about the honor of a southern gentleman and what he must do.

In the weeks and months following the caning, those who assailed Brooks decried the use of force against an unarmed, seated man whose only crime was to use strong words to defend Kansas and attack slavery. For those who defended Brooks and blamed Sumner, the "Crime against Kansas" speech was a body blow that cried out for punishment. To add insult to Sumner's injury, his opponents called into question everything from the seriousness of his wounds to how he had cowered and moaned in unmanly fashion under the blows. In summary, the reactions in the House and Senate mirrored exactly the divisions over the extension of slavery.

Congress Deliberates

Sumner's friend, Senator Henry Wilson, who had conveyed the bloodied abolitionist to his lodgings immediately after the assault, led the call for an official inquiry into the assault. There was little doubt as to their objective. They wanted sanctions against Brooks. They needed to make the case against him both in the public eye and officially, and they sought justice for their friend. However, they also wanted to avoid looking overly political. When Wilson's moderate request for Senate action met with little support, Seward called for a committee.

The Senate appointed a committee consisting of Philip Allen of Rhode Island, Lewis Cass of Michigan, Henry Dodge of Wisconsin, James A. Pearce of Maryland, and Henry S. Geyer of Missouri to investigate the question. Without a single Republican in its membership, it reported on May 28 that the Senate did not have the authority under the Constitution to discipline a member or members of the House. Regardless, in many ways, the report was a victory for the Republicans, for it cast the matter into the hands of the House, and there the Republicans had the influence and the speakership. In addition, the report noted that Sumner was seated and that Brooks did "assault him with considerable violence." It was not as favorable as it could have been. It attributed the cause of the attack to "certain language used by Mr. Sumner in debate."[10]

During the Senate debate on the committee report, on May 27, there was an incident that is instructive. In the midst of reflecting the manner of the attack, Wilson described the assault as follows: "Mr. Sumner was stricken down on this floor by a brutal, murderous, and cowardly assault"—but he got no further. Although his exclamation was removed from the *Globe* with unanimous consent, Butler was heard as shouting "You are a liar!" The president pro tempore of the Senate, Jesse D. Bright, a Democrat from Indiana, ruled that Wilson's words were "unparliamentary." Butler had already requested that his own interjection be stricken from the *Globe*. Despite whatever truth may have been in those words—after all, the assault was brutal, possibly murderous in intent, and might easily be construed as cowardly considering the victim was seated and unarmed—the Senate still had rules about proper language. One could not help but sympathize with Ohio Senator Benjamin Franklin Wade's sentiments, expressed earlier in the discussion: "If the principle now announced here is to prevail, let us come armed for the combat; and although you [Democrats] are four to one, I am here to meet you."[11]

Wilson later recalled, in his history of the events, that Brooks had challenged him to a duel in response to his characterization of the assault. He declined the invitation, stating, "I have always regarded dueling as the lingering relic of a barbarous civilization, which the law of the country has branded a crime." He learned, in 1873, from Representative James L. Orr of South Carolina, former Speaker of the House, that it was only Orr's advice to southern congressmen at a meeting at the National Hotel that saved Wilson from an assault of a similar nature as that which befell Sumner.[12]

On May 23, one day after the assault, the House appointed a committee of Ohioan Lewis D. Campbell, Opposition Party, who had proposed the investigation; New Yorker Francis E. Spinner, then a Democrat but a future Republican; New Jerseyan Alexander C. M. Pennington, Opposition Party (the three of whom formed the majority of the committee); and former Georgia governor Howell Cobb and Speaker of the House Alfred B. Greenwood from Arkansas, both Democrats and, coincidentally, graduates of the University of Georgia. On June 2, the House Investigating Committee in the Case of the

Assault on Mr. Sumner gave its reports, majority and minority, and released the testimony it had gathered.

Although the two reports agreed on the material facts, their views on every issue involved were opposites. The majority found that the House had the authority to discipline Brooks and whoever else was involved; that the assault was unwarranted as Sumner had made a lawful speech protected under the Constitution; that Brooks, Keitt, and Edmundson violated their duties to refrain from such activity, or in Edmundson's case, to warn the authorities and try to prevent the violence; and that the assault "asserts for physical force a prerogative over governments, constitutions, and laws; and, if carried to its ultimate consequences, must result in anarchy, and bring in its train all the evils of a 'reign of terror.'" They recommended expulsion for Brooks and censure for Keitt and Edmundson.[13]

The minority report declared the reverse. First of all, it referred only to the "alleged assault" even though Brooks never denied that he assaulted Sumner and, in fact, confessed to it multiple times in signed documents. Second, it applied the criminal protections of the Bill of Rights to the proceedings of the House in spite of the language of Article I, Section Five, Clause 2, of the Constitution: "Each House may determine the rules of its proceedings, punish its members for disorderly behavior, and, with the concurrence of two thirds, expel a member." The minority had failed to distinguish between office-holding, a privilege, and liability for deprivations due to the commission of a crime. Third, it declared that the above clause referred only to conduct within each House pursuant to its official business.

The minority concluded that the House of Representatives did not have the authority to punish any of its members for what they did outside of the House of Representatives. It was a strained reading of the clause. It defied prior precedent, not the least of which was the Houston-Stanbery case, in which Houston was censured. Joshua Giddings of Ohio too was censured in 1842 for offering resolutions that slave rebels were only acting according to their natural law rights. The minority report defied logic by arguing that the House could not expel or punish a member for activity outside of the House. The House had the power to refuse to seat a member, although election to such a seat took place outside of the House—sometimes thousands of miles away.

The testimony the committee gathered is the most comprehensive single record we have of the assault. Neither Brooks nor Keitt testified in any form other than, in Brooks's case, a letter to the Senate. Counting the two affidavits from the Senate's inquiry included in the House report, there were twenty-seven people who gave their version of events, including the assault itself, what they heard before or after, and, in the case of the two doctors, the type and severity of the injuries. Besides the two doctors, most of the interviewees were congressmen. The remaining six were a doorkeeper of the House, two sergeants at arms, two journalists, and a secretary to the legation in Peru, who was a former captain in the Maryland contingent in the Mexican-American War.

The witnesses agreed on several details: Sumner was seated at the start, Brooks inflicted several blows, the assault was premeditated, and Sumner received bloody injury. They disagreed on some points, including whether Sumner dislodged his desk, his conduct during the beating, Keitt's role in the event, and the severity of Sumner's injuries. This is expected. The literature on witness reliability demonstrates that even those with a clear view of an event will confabulate, interpret, and rework the details into a memory they will recall with a certainty even though much of the detail is the product of their mind's inner workings. This does not even take account of the fact that people see, hear, and sense from a set of rules colored by their own experience, culture, and deeply held prejudices.

When one adds to the difficulties with eyewitness evidence concussion and blood loss, even Charles Sumner's recounting of the event becomes problematic. For example, consider his observations of the events after he regained consciousness: "Others there were at a distance, looking on, and offering no assistance, of whom I recognized only Mr. Douglas, of Illinois, Mr. Toombs, of Georgia, and I thought also my assailant, standing between them." Douglas and Toombs, upon learning of this statement, denied any such close proximity to each other or Brooks in the moments after the attack. Douglas asserted, "I was not near Mr. Brooks; I did not enter the room till some minutes after the affray was over." Toombs concurred, "As to what Mr. Sumner says about Mr. Brooks standing between myself and the Senator from Illinois, there is not a word of truth in it."[14]

They did admit to not aiding Sumner or making any moves to render assistance after the fact. In short, they behaved exactly as they did in politics. They stood by and took no action to arrest the violence. They expressed no sympathy for the victim. They exhibited no camaraderie for their fellow senator. One wonders what their feelings might have been had Sumner died. It would be a sad commentary indeed if they blamed the victim and his politics as they did for the assault, although blaming the victim is one strategy that defense lawyers in murder trials often assay.

In addition to arguing that Sumner had caused the attack, invited the violence, and deserved his beating, Brooks and his supporters argued that Sumner's ailments were not all that serious. For this conclusion they relied on Brooks's statement in criminal court and elsewhere that his first blow was "but a tap" and the conclusions of Dr. Cornelius Boyle, who made the initial dressing of Sumner's wounds, that the wounds were not serious. "I look upon them as flesh wounds." Boyle reached this conclusion in spite of the fact that the two wounds that required dressing were cuts to the bone of Sumner's skull. He also determined that Sumner was fit to return to the Senate despite the fact that he had been rendered unconscious by one of the blows and had considerable blood loss. Because he found no sign that the blows had ruptured an artery, he did not think the blows could lead to death.[15] The committee members did not see fit to ask the surgeon whether Sumner's subsequent infection, as indicated by his high fever, was of any concern. Although the notion of sepsis was already well established in medicine, Boyle had made no effort to cleanse the wounds with an antiseptic before dressing them. He might have introduced the germs himself, if his hands or his instruments were not clean.

Inherent in their accusations of Sumner's "shamming" was the southern view of Sumner as both a liar and something less than a man, in other words a slave, an appropriate target for thrashing. Boyle gave them plenty of ammunition in his testimony. "His wounds do not necessarily confine him one moment . . . There are a great many friends present, and they make Mr. Sumner out a great deal worse than he is." Boyle denied the existence of any trauma, although after such a beating, the body would naturally go into shock. Shock is itself dangerous, with the head being denied its proper blood supply. But an observer indifferent to this process might describe Sumner's posture as fainting, then associated with female weakness or male cowardice. When questioned on the subject of his own political views, Boyle declared himself an "old-line Whig, if I have any politics," and that he did not treat patients with regard to their politics.[16] For the Republicans, Boyle's medical judgment was a critical blow to their cause. Who could make Sumner a martyr if he merely fainted?

What had generally gone unnoticed except by Sumner's ardent defenders was the testimony of former captain Nathan Darling, who had dressed wounds in the Mexican-American War. He stated, "I believe, if the licks had been struck with half the force on another part of the head, they would have killed him instantly."[17] Fortunately for Sumner, they had fallen on the crown, the thickest part of his skull. This impression had been confirmed to a degree by Boyle— only the phrasing of the question led Boyle to emphasize the lack of seriousness of the blows rather than the seriousness of the attack as a threat to Sumner's life. Brooks had come very close to committing murder, rather than a mere thrashing.

If we are to compare the medical evidence with Brooks's statements about his intent, we are left with two possibilities: either he did not know his own strength or much about thrashing, or he lost control of himself. We must remember that Crittenden shouted "Don't kill him!" and that Brooks was restrained from further hitting Sumner even after the blows rendered Sumner unconscious and he had fallen to the floor.

The committee also questioned Dr. M. S. Perry, the physician Wilson and other friends of Sumner brought in when they became suspicious of Boyle's lack of concern for his patient's complaints. Perry had seen Sumner on Wednesday, May 28, and observed that "suppuration had taken place in the wounds on the right side of his head" and Sumner had a considerable fever.[18] This meant that pus filled the wounds and Sumner was fighting off a systemic (as opposed to a local) infection. Local infections cause pain, swelling, redness, and discharge. Systemic infections can kill. Given that Boyle was unlikely to have used sterile equipment to dress the wounds or cleaned them before treatment, standard medical practice at the time, this situation would not be unexpected, but it also indicates that Sumner was suffering from not just the cuts, the bleeding, and the immediate impact of the blows but the aftereffects as well.

We cannot know for certain the extent, seriousness, or permanency (if any) of damage that may have resulted from Brooks's assault. After receiving such blows and having Sumner's complaints of head pain, lack of steadiness on his feet, nervous exhaustion, and difficulty with physical exertion, a current medical patient would have received X-rays and possibly an MRI and likely would have been diagnosed as having a concussion. Concussions are classed as simple and complex. In the former, the symptoms resolve themselves with rest within one or two weeks. There is no loss of functional abilities. In the latter, the symptoms—pain, disorientation, weakness, dizziness, and even loss of mental and physical skills—persist and may flare up in severity long after the concussion occurred.

The persistence of Sumner's symptoms might indicate anything from a subdural hematoma—bleeding on the brain—to post-concussion syndrome. The infection and fever might well have created a permanent neurological disorder. Then again, the Pulitzer Prize–winning biography may be right about Sumner's problems being post-traumatic stress disorder, a psychological ailment from a highly disturbing incident. In other words, this is another way of saying that the injuries were not physical, but primarily psychological. However, just because symptoms are psychological does not make them any less real. Regardless of the situation, Sumner would not return to his Senate duties full-time until 1860.

Butler and Keitt were able to remain in Congress for a time, but they faced more than just accusatory speeches. The House committee had recommended expulsion for Butler and censure for Keitt and Edmundson. While debating whether Brooks merited expulsion, their colleagues also exchanged remarks about Keitt's and Edmundson's share of the blame, if any. Although Northerners dominated in the House, even if they voted as a block (highly unlikely considering Democrats in the North were unlikely to vote out one of their own), they still would not have the two-thirds majority necessary for Brooks's expulsion, and censure did little or nothing. When the votes finally did come at the end of the session, they did not surprise. A majority, but not the required two-thirds, voted in favor of expulsion for Brooks, an unimportant censure for Keitt, and against censure for Edmundson, who had successfully pleaded that he could not be compelled "to turn traitor to my friend."[19]

In spite of the fact that the votes did not affect their situations in the slightest, Brooks and Keitt made the grand gesture: they resigned, but not before giving substantial addresses on the incident on July 14 and 16, respectively. Assured of reelection, they had little to fear. The House allowed them to proceed. Their supposed disgrace did not interfere with the privileges they had denied to Sumner by beating him into disability.

Brooks made several points that showed that he neither regretted nor accepted sanction for his actions. He declared Sumner's speech to be a "libel" of both his state and "his blood." It was a "personal affair," and he felt duty bound to defend South Carolina, saying "I hope I shall always be prepared, humbly and modestly, to perform the duty of a son."[20] Further, he argued that only the Senate had the ability to properly punish him, along with the criminal courts if he were prosecuted. His presentation made the principles of a southern gentleman clear. Everything involving them was a point of honor. Politics quickly became personal.

Besides setting up the dangerous precedent that Senator Wade declared to be the beginning of anarchy, Brooks was advocating a curious version of the law of libel. Libel or defamation held that publishing a falsehood that resulted in damage to a reputation was punishable by law for damages. First, if the speech was indeed libelous, only Butler could have sued in court because only Butler was specifically mentioned, not Brooks. But even Butler's suit would have been dismissed because Sumner's "Crime against Kansas" heaped obloquy on Butler and South Carolina, but it did not make false statements. But again, the word *libel* in the southern lexicon of honor did not mean the same as *libel* in the common-law books. To libel a gentleman was to call into question his motives or to bring low his reputation, and this might be done by published truth as much as be spreading falsehoods.

By contrast, Brooks's justification for his actions as stemming from a type of filial duty reveals a great deal more than he probably intended. Keeping in mind that he dueled Wigfall as a second when the primaries exchanged shots ineffectively because Wigfall had posted his father, Brooks's understanding of the honor culture was so thoroughly intertwined with personal emotions—the proclivities of an intemperate son and brother—as to form a concoction of seething, righteous certitude. If he felt that honor demanded he act, no act was beyond the pale.

All the same, he peppered his speech with humor, wit, and legal precedent, and it was well received. Although he had bludgeoned a fellow human being, who was unarmed and a senator, into unconsciousness, his audience treated Brooks's address with respect, laughing at his jokes and the final figurative swipes he took at his victim.

Laurence M. Keitt was treated in much the same manner, although he had done little more than incite Brooks the day before the caning and, during the event, threaten the venerable Senator John J. Crittenden with a cane for daring to tell Brooks not to kill Sumner. One scholar very astutely finds it credible that Keitt had been the moving force behind Brooks all along. After all, not only was Keitt the more prominent brawler, but he was very vocal in defense of South Carolina, slavery, and the South and a vigorous attacker of free-soil advocates. His vision of a vast southern empire of slavery had been turned into a land of depravity, rape of African-American women, and bar-

barity in Sumner's oration. It is highly likely that he resented his secondary role in the affair.

As was Keitt's wont, he used his time during the speech entitled "Defense of South Carolina" to both praise South Carolina and hurl invective at abolitionists and Massachusetts, at one point calling "Fred Douglas," William Lloyd Garrison, and "Abby Folsom" "lepers of history." Of Massachusetts's role in the American Revolution, he declared, "Her prosperity mainly resting upon the African slave trade, loans of money to the enemy in time of war, and smuggling, well may she bedeck herself with finery."[21] Apparently, South Carolinians could engage in their own fierce rhetoric but could not abide it hurled against themselves.

It is not unexpected that Keitt would defend South Carolina against Sumner's charges. His reason for assaulting Massachusetts and abolitionism in the course of defending South Carolina's contribution to the revolution is less clear, except when one looks at the speech in the context of contemporary politics. This was not a dispute about American history; this was about the current political, economic situation. Keitt saw himself and his state on the losing side of a nationwide struggle over power, resources, and status. Unlike Brooks, Keitt had made no secret of his secessionist tendencies. If anything, he was Brooks times ten. Like a cornered animal, he struck out with a passion ill fitting his actual situation, one of strength and security.

Brooks in Court

Brooks did not just stand accused in the court of Congress. After the assault he faced legal proceedings. Just after leaving the Senate floor, Brooks presented himself to Judge Hollingshead to tender his bond for any subsequent criminal prosecution. Hollingshead released him without bond as the action was premature. On the sworn statement of an eyewitness to the assault, William Y. Leader of Philadelphia, Hollingshead later issued an arrest warrant for Brooks. Oddly, contemporary historians have ignored Leader's account, which was published in 1875 in *The Works of Charles Sumner*, instead preferring to rely solely on the House investigating committee's report, various statements in the *Congressional Globe*, and Brooks's unpublished writings. While some have cited newspaper stories, those newspapers were more likely than not drawing their reports from documents like Leader's statement to Hollingshead.

All the same, Leader's account of the events makes interesting reading. First, Leader revealed that he was but a few feet from the incident, allowing him to overhear Brooks's remarks and observe firsthand what followed. Second, Leader reported that Brooks began to strike before he completed the last sentence of his declaration. Third, Sumner did not attempt to rise to "defend himself," but only attempted to evade the blows. Fourth, Sumner was already on the ground, having dislodged his desk, when Brooks broke his cane over him. Fifth, Leader noted, "a number of persons gathered around, crying, 'Don't interfere!' 'Go it, Brooks!' 'Give the damned Abolitionists hell!' &c." Sixth, it was Crittenden who first got to Brooks and restrained him from further violence. Seventh, Leader claimed not to know Sumner and "as we belonged to different political parties, I had no prejudice in his favor." He summarized his assessment of the proceedings as "the most cold-blooded, high-handed outrages ever committed" and concluded that had Sumner not been "a very large and powerfully built man, it must have resulted in his death."[22] From this viewpoint, the incident appears to be a clear-cut case of assault and battery with aggravating circumstances (the use of a weapon).

After his arrest, Brooks spent little to no time in jail. He was immediately freed on bail of five hundred dollars. But the grand jury indicted him, and he faced a bench trial before Judge Thomas H. Crawford of the Circuit Court for the District of Columbia. Following a very brief hearing, on July 8, Crawford sentenced Brooks to a fine of three hundred dollars. The light sentence, with no incarceration, caused a new wave of outrage among Sumner's sympathizers. Had the court simply vindicated the honor culture? The law can be a mystery unless one looks closely at its operations.

The outcome of a trial is the result of several factors, including the provisions under which one is prosecuted, the effectiveness of the prosecutor, the judge's rulings, and the effectiveness of one's defense. Without getting into an intensive analysis of the antebellum American criminal justice system, there are a few observations that come to mind. First and foremost is the fact that laws reflect the values of societies. The societies of Washington, D.C., and Maryland produced the laws governing this trial. As noted above, it was an area very friendly to, if not entirely stemming from, the honor culture of the slaveholding South. Second, the outcome depended heavily on the conduct of the prosecutor. The prosecutor did not represent Sumner, the alleged victim. The prosecutor, in this case the U.S. Attorney for Washington, D.C., represented the government, or, as it was commonly phrased, the people.

Brooks was most fortunate in this regard because the U.S. Attorney was a presidential appointment and the president, Franklin Pierce, no friend of Sumner, had appointed Maryland Democrat Philip Barton Key. Barton, as he was known in Washington, D.C.'s best circles, was as close as one could be to Washington, D.C., royalty. His father, Francis Scott Key, more noted as the author of "The Star-Spangled Banner," was the U.S. Attorney for Washington, D.C., under President Jackson. Barton's sister was the belle of Washington, D.C., society and the wife of Representative George H. Pendleton, Democrat from Ohio, who, as a senator, would author the Civil Service Act of 1883 that bears his name. His uncle, the husband of his father's sister, was Chief Justice Roger B. Taney, who was then in the twentieth year of what would be the second longest term as chief justice. Taney's "self-inflicted wound" in *Dred Scott v. Sanford* (1857)—Congress could not bar slavery from the territories, and Americans of African ancestry could never be citizens—lay in the future, but the chief justice had already proved himself a good friend to the slave power.

Barton himself was the dashing, womanizing, states' rights Democratic darling of Washington, D.C. He was better known for his dancing, conversation, and the figure he cut riding his horse, Lucifer, than his attention to his duties at the office. It was Key's decision not to charge Brooks with a more serious offense. It was also Key's choice not to challenge Brooks's speech on his own behalf. Finally, Key chose to read into evidence the letters he and Sumner had exchanged on why Sumner could not be present in the court to give his testimony. Although Key may have been legitimately trying to excuse Sumner's absence and demonstrate his own due diligence, it was a tactical blunder in that it made Sumner look like he was feigning incapacity. However, the testimony of Doctors Boyle and Lindsay alongside that of the other eyewitnesses, including Leader, should have been more than enough to allay that suspicion. One suspects Key's motives in such an affair—an affair in which he had no sympathy for the victim and great admiration for the defendant.

After the farcical trial of Brooks, Key gained infamy as the unsuccessful prosecutor of California Representative Philemon T. Herbert for killing an Irish waiter by the name of Thomas Keating at the popular Willard's Hotel. Key made little effort to produce witnesses for the prosecution to show that Keating was not armed when Herbert had instigated the struggle, a struggle that led to Herbert shooting Keating. But Key's most infamous role came on February 27, 1859, when he played the murder victim of Congressman "Dangerous" Dan Sickles. In what may be poetic justice, the jury would acquit Sickles of all charges because Sickles pleaded temporary insanity. He had found Key signaling to Sickles's wife, Teresa, outside their Washington, D.C., house, apparently in an attempt to see if the house was clear for an assignation. In another coincidence, the presiding judge in the trial was none other than Thomas H. Crawford, the judge in Brooks's trial. He, too, played his customary role, giving favorable rulings for Sickles's defense of "irresistible impulse."

Brooks also had a very effective defense team at his trial. In addition to his primary counsel, John A. Linton, he also had James L. Orr to represent him. Toombs and Senator Judah P. Benjamin of Louisiana testified for the defense. Toombs read portions of the "Crime against Kansas" speech—out of context—that demeaned Butler and South Carolina. Benjamin asserted that copies of the speech were printed beforehand, suggesting that Sumner was the culprit of a premeditated offense. How the passages of the speech were relevant as a defense or that publication in advance somehow excused Brooks is unclear, unless Brooks wanted to anticipate Sickles's defense of temporary insanity. And Brooks wanted none of that. Moreover, both Toombs and Benjamin sought political capital rather than evidentiary clarity. In effect, they were riding Brooks's popular coattails to reelection in their own states.

Brooks concluded the defense's presentation with his own speech. As this was a bench trial, he need only appeal to Judge Crawford's sense of the law. There was no jury to sway. A Polk appointee to the Circuit Court of the District of Columbia, he was a Jacksonian Democrat, a graduate of Princeton, a two-term congressman from Pennsylvania, a former Commissioner of Indian Affairs, and had been on the court since 1845. Brooks knew that Crawford was a "doughface"—a southern-leaning Northerner—from his role in the case of the *Pearl*. The *Pearl* was a slave ship marooned in Washington, D.C., after the slaves had attempted to commandeer her. Crawford apparently believed that color alone determined whether a man was a slave.

Brooks began by lamenting Sumner's absence from the proceedings—a sarcastic reference to the supposed seriousness of his injuries. Brooks contended that the first blow was "but a tap, and intended to put him on his guard," as opposed to Sumner's contention that the first blow "stunned" him "so as to lose sight." Brooks spent the vast majority of the rest of his statement on the notion that some acts that violate laws are nevertheless not appropriate for punishment: "So also are those cases which may fall under the condemnation of the letter of the law, and yet like considerations will restrain its penalties." He declared his premeditated bludgeoning a matter of "feeling" that was not covered by the "reasoning" of law. It would be unjust to punish him severely for what was natural. "Will it be required that I, with a heart to feel and an arm to strike, shall patiently hear and ignobly submit while my political mother is covered with insult and obloquy, and dishonor? while her character is slandered, and her reputation libeled?"[23]

In some respects, Brooks was using an excuse for crime known as "irresistible impulse" or crime of passion. Under this doctrine, if someone acted in the heat of the moment driven by an emotional response that could not be controlled, he or she did not have the requisite control over his or her actions required to form intent. Intent is the state of mind necessary to be held responsible for one's actions. Just as we would not find that an arm moved by gravity is under the control of the person to whom it is attached, we would not find Brooks responsible for actions driven by human responses beyond his control. The most frequently used example of this defense is when a spouse finds his or her partner in a sexual act with another and harms one or both of them. Unfortunately for Brooks's use of irresistible impulse as a defense, he had read the speech the day before the assault. This was more than enough time to constitute the "cooling off period" that vitiates the irresistible impulse defense.

Crawford pronounced the sentence of the court without comment on the evidence as "this matter will be within a short time the subject of investigation in another place,"[24] probably referring to the House investigation. Crawford seemed to think that anything the House would decide would be more appropriate than his own decision, a strange opinion for a judge to render. According to all accounts, Brooks paid his fine of three hundred dollars and walked free.

Despite the substantial fine, which was the equivalent of roughly seventy-five hundred dollars today, from his issuance of challenges to Wilson and Representative Anson Burlingame after the assault on Sumner, we may conclude that he was not chastised in the slightest. Burlingame accepted Brooks's challenge but chose Canada as the place for the encounter. Brooks, either fearing traveling through the North—his official reason—or well knowing Burlingame's reputation as a marksman, declined. His private letters to his brother on May 23 and June 21 reveal a similar bravado mixed with a concern about his fate. They also show his public speeches to be much more moderate than his feelings of the time.

Besides referring to "Black Republicans" in his second letter, he let his true sentiments be known: "They [abolitionists] are making all sorts of threats. It would not take much to have the throats of every Abolitionist cut." As for the blows he struck, "Every lick went where I intended." His motive was to stand in the place of the aggrieved Butler because "Sumner is a very powerful man and weighs 30 pounds more than myself." He also confessed to having sought Sumner on May 21 unsuccessfully, and then, on the next day, after waiting in the same place on the Capitol grounds for an hour and a half, he went into the chamber. Again he claimed to have given his short speech to Sumner before commencing the attack. He went on to confess that "At the concluding words I struck him with my cane and gave him about 30 first rate stripes with a gutta percha cane which had been given me a few months before by a friend from N Carolina named Vick [?]." He took joy in his accomplishment of having beaten Sumner unconscious, writing that "Towards the last he bellowed like a calf."[25]

Several conclusions come from these letters. First, Brooks intended to punish Sumner publicly. Second, he regarded Sumner's speech as "violent." Third, he was intimidated by Sumner's size. Fourth, he had carefully planned the attack to compensate for his deficiencies in relation to his object—he did not want Sumner to be able to defend himself. Fifth, he took pleasure and pride in what he had done. Sixth, although he had some fear of "assassination," he believed that all would be well and he would emerge unscathed.[26] On this last point he was sorely mistaken. Finally, the "30" strokes was considerably more than he admitted in Congress or in court—making him either a perjurer in the former or a liar to his kinfolk.

There is one other document that merits consideration. In Brooks's hand and with his signature, there is a narrative entitled "Statement of Mr. Brooks" dated May 28, 1856. As this was at the same time as the House committee was investigating the incident, he may have been preparing testimony ahead of their questions. It diverges from his other remarks and others' testimony in several respects. It also reinforces the impression that he planned the assault exactly as it turned out.

First, he admitted striking Sumner before completing his declaration. Second, he confessed that he had to "strike him harder than I intended" on the second blow when Sumner attempted to rise, or in Brooks's words, "endeavoured to make a battle." Third, he claimed to have moderated his strikes after the fifth when Sumner "ceased to resist." Fourth, he recounted that Crittenden had "took hold of me and said something like 'dont kill him.'" Fifth, he denied hitting Sumner after he fell. Sixth, he asserted, although Emundson, Orr, and Keitt knew of his plan, that they had not accompanied him or played any role in the matter. Brooks did add the admission that he had selected "an ordinary walking stick made of gutta percha and hollow" because "it was light and elastic and because I fancied it would not break."[27] The latter was his only miscalculation.

Newspaper Verdicts

The impact of the affair was not confined to its principal figures or to Congress and the court in Washington, D.C. Less than a day after the caning, newspapers both North and South were reporting the event. It rapidly spread beyond an altercation between two men in Washington, D.C., and became one of the first mass media events. While we today are familiar with the instant, twenty-four-hour news cycle, for America in 1856 the concept of immediate news was very new. In many respects the form of this new mass media shaped the controversy that followed. There were two developments driving the way newspapers reported the event and those that followed that deserve our notice.

First, there was the arrival of the telegraph. Through a national network of electrical wires, electrical impulses in a code of dashes and dots traversed the country. This allowed for the nearly instantaneous transmission of messages from city to city across vast spaces. The more urban areas were better served by the telegraph than more rural places, but both North and South were still largely rural. It also does not mean that the information traveling along those wires was true or even well conceived. The transmission was only as accurate as the report it translated into those impulses. What was not in doubt was the rapid spread of this technology. From 1844, when Samuel F. B. Morse first demonstrated his device by sending a message from Washington, D.C., to Baltimore, to 1852, the nation had strung up seventeen thousand miles of wire and linked up every major metropolitan center to the others except for San Francisco. By 1860, it would be fifty thousand miles of wire. In addition, in order to deal with the costs of the magnetic telegraph, a group of the largest New York papers formed the Associated Press in 1849 and laid another cornerstone of modern journalism.

The second major development in the distribution of news was the arrival of the steam-powered rotary press in the late 1840s. In the 1830s a newspaper using the most modern equipment could produce 250 sheets per hour, double sided. With a steam-powered rotary press, a newspaper company with a full-page, four-page newspaper could print five to ten thousand copies an hour. With this advance in printing came the problems of a modern industrial firm. The startup costs involved also increased apace from a mere five hundred to a thousand dollars to create a newspaper in the 1830s to the hundreds of thousands of dollars required by the 1850s. Additionally, one needed to sell copies in quantities that made up for this capital investment at a rate that was competitive. With higher production capacity, unit costs came down, but this meant the need to sell tens of thousands of papers instead of hundreds or thousands. Furthermore, competition in the newspaper business during the 1850s was fierce.

It was not the industry we know today as journalism or, more derogatorily, infotainment. Professional reporters were also relatively new, and the papers themselves were still highly partisan affairs. The census of 1860 categorized 80 percent of the newspapers as "political in their character."[28] In addition to being affiliated with political parties, newspapers went with their owner's personal allegiances. The papers of one political party might easily be divided into supporting different wings of the party or even bosses within the wings of a political party.

Then, there was the sheer number of newspapers. By 1860 there were 3,725 papers, of which 387 were dailies, with a total circulation of 888 million copies. Put another way, there were 28.2 copies per American. However, we should note that the vast majority of newspapers were in the more literate North, which had achieved 80 percent white adult male literacy by 1860. These conditions created fierce competition among newspapers for readers. They competed not just about who could land the story first but about who could tell the most interesting story in both words and, through woodblock prints, pictures.

As a result, newspapers had just as much reason as any other media or entertainment organization to drum up controversy and celebrity and to paint the story in the most colorful way possible. It has become common practice to lament the decline in civility in news media coverage, in political advertising, and among commentators. In a world in which media conglomerates fight with each other, blogs try to outdo one another in stridency, and Americans seek out the news venues that reflect their political views, many observers regret the lack of objectivity. Yet, they would find that the world of the 1850s made the present look like a tea party by comparison.

There were other reasons newspapers played their part in the Brooks-Sumner incident. Whether they were aware of it or not, they were the practitioners, purveyors, and sculptors of public values, or at least prevailing notions of proper behavior, identity, and morality. While individual newspapers may have had the realities of journalism and mass media markets in common, they differed based on what population constituted their readership, provided their personnel, and gave them their material. You could predict the reactions of a newspaper based on its affiliation, and they had some striking similarities that affected the nature of the crisis.

All of the papers examined for this study issued an editorial response in addition to the telegraph message reporting on the incident from Washington, D.C. They also agreed that the conflict was serious and used strong language to describe the assault. Although follow-ups within a few days of the first reports clarified and added detail, the news was treated as urgent and of great import. On all other matters, disagreements erupted. Republican, Democrat, and American Party editorials in the North and border states agreed that the attack was "brutal," inappropriate in its location, and improper. Northern language was more condemnatory of Brooks as a "brute" and exculpatory of Sumner's use of language in the "Crime against Kansas" speech. Democratic commentaries tended to focus more on what Sumner had done to provoke it, while the American Party and southern Whig comments maintained a more balanced approach.[29]

In the North, writers emphasized the protection of freedom of speech. The Indianapolis, Indiana, *Locomotive* in a piece entitled "Freedom of Speech" on May 23 declared the following: "Freedom of speech should be guarantied to all public men in debate on public questions, and the spirit of ruffianism exhibited by Brooks cannot be too highly censured." In keeping with its Democratic Party affiliation, it also stated, "This is another result of the bitter personal partisan spirit, that characterizes the press and public speakers of the day, and while it continues, will excite men to acts of lawless outrages that they would not think of in calmer moments." Understandably, the Republican paper in Boston, the *Atlas*, was much more belligerent in its language in a May 23 editorial: "The reign of terror, then, is to be transferred to Washington, and the mouths of the representatives of the North are to be closed by the use of bowie-knives, bludgeons, and revolvers. Very well; the sooner we understand this the better."

At the same time, some Republican papers rejected the honor culture entirely in favor of another conception of manhood. On May 24, the Buffalo, New York, *Morning Express* editorialized: "He [Sumner] had dashed them down beneath his feet like pigmies, and burning with mortification at their abasement in the eyes of the world, brute force was resorted to, to accomplish by the blows of a club what they could not do by the power of intellect." This notion of the brutalization of men by slavery, who in turn brutalized others, was a key theme of abolitionist advocacy that now found new life in the denunciation of Brooks's attack.

Although Whig and Democratic papers in the North paid due attention to Sumner's provocative speech as the cause, they too denounced the attack. Boston's Whig paper, the *Courier*, chose to do so in the terms of the honor culture on May 23: "The member from South Carolina transgressed every rule of honor which should animate or restrain one gentleman in his connections with another, in his ruffian assault upon Mr. Sumner. There is no chivalry in a brute. There is no manliness in a scoundrel." The Republican New York *Tribune* of May 23 made a similar point, but it also echoed some of the arguments Southerners used about northern threats: "If, indeed, we go on quietly to submit to such outrages, we deserve to have our names flattened, our skins blacked, and to be placed at work under task-masters; for we have lost the noblest attributes of freemen, and are virtually slaves." Even in their outrage over the assault, Republicans exhibited a similar racism to that of their cousins from the South.

More common to the Democratic papers in the North was the call for calm. In doing so, they condemned both the assault and the speech they argued had provoked it. They needed only to draw on their well-worn disapprobation for Sumner and all of his previous speeches. Embedded within these balanced appraisals was a notion of fair play. As the Cincinnati *Daily Enquirer* put it on May 23, "In short, those who play at *bowls* must expect *rubbers!*"

This line of reasoning became even more pronounced as the newspapers began to brawl with one another over their respective positions on the assault. On May 26, the Boston *Courier* responded to the *Atlas* criticism by arguing, "The object of the *Atlas* is to obtain personal and political capital from

SOUTHERN CHIVALRY — ARGUMENT versus CLUB'S.

"Southern Chivalry—Argument versus Club's." J. L. Magee, Lithograph, 1856. Print Collection, Miriam and Ira D. Wallach Division of Art, Prints and Photographs, The New York Public Library, Astor, Lenox, and Tilden Foundations.

the occurrence at Washington, and as a party paper, it is only performing legitimate business in endeavoring to turn the tide of indignation into its own mill-stream." While we cannot determine for certain whether their exchange of words affected the larger public view, it is likely that these continuing disputes kept the issue alive, vigorous, and hotly contested.

Southern Democratic editorials were almost all in favor of what Brooks had done and used strong language against Sumner, including calling him a "coward" for his "Crime against Kansas" speech; therefore, Brooks's attack was appropriate. They engaged in what contemporary commentators have called the "blame the victim" strategy. In these editorials Sumner deserved it for his provocative language, his ungentlemanly behavior, and, more importantly, his targeting of the elderly and absent Butler. He also came under attack for his lack of manliness as Brooks's remark about him "bellowing like a calf" at the end gained wide circulation.

Historians have disagreed over the extent of the unity of opinion among these southern commentaries, some arguing for some editorials being critical of the place of the attack, others asserting a consensus around the fundamentals of the need for and praiseworthiness of Brooks's action. In that southern editorials agreed that Sumner deserved a punishment, both are correct.[30] The Louisville, Kentucky, *Journal*, an American Party newspaper, looked askance at both Brooks and South Carolina. "This only proves," it declared on May 28, "that, bad as the representative may be, he is no worse than the State he represents."

Proving the point, the Yorkville, South Carolina, *Enquirer*, while it regretted the necessity of the assault, offered praise for Brooks on May 29: "No better or more gallant man could have been selected to begin the argument; and because he has thus begun it so thoroughly, we give him an unstinted commendation. Well done!" These sentiments were uttered in different papers throughout the Deep South, such as the Milledgeville, Georgia, *Federal Union*, which on June 3 condemned Massachusetts as well for protesting the assault: "Whilst she refuses to submit to the laws of the Union, she cannot claim the protection of those laws for her Senators, and whilst she chooses to be represented in the U.S. Senate by blackguards, she ought not to complain if they receive a blackguard's reward."

The comments about the affair did not quickly die down. Each new development, whether it was Brooks's challenge to Wilson and then Burlingame, or the arrival of fresh testimony, or the outcome of the trial and vote on expulsion, added to the flurry of words both North and South. In this fashion, newspapers continually stirred, reflected on, and brought energy to the debate that emerged on the propriety of the assault, its larger meaning, the fairness of the outcome, Sumner's true condition, and what the events portended for the future of the Union. For example, the Richmond, Virginia, *Whig*, then an American Party paper despite its name, asserted on May 31 that Sumner and his political partners were faking the injuries for political effect: "[W]e believe it is a miserable Abolition trick from beginning to end—resorted to to keep alive and diffuse and strengthen the sympathy awakened for him among his confederates at the North. Nigger-worshipping fanatics of the male gender, and weak-minded women and silly children, are horribly affected at the thought of blood oozing out from a pin-scratch. And Sumner is wily politician enough to take advantage of this little fact."

Keeping in mind that caricatures were restricted to the North due to the South's honor culture's objection to the form, several notable artistic renderings of the affair contributed to this swirl of emotion. Homer Winslow cre-

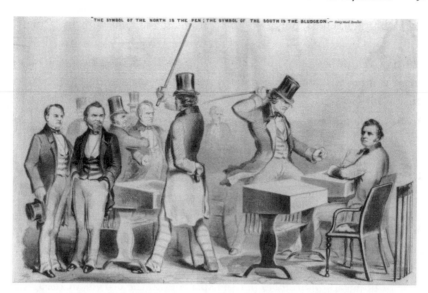

"Argument of the Chivalry." A print, possibly by Winslow Homer, depicting the caning, with, from left to right, Senators Robert Toombs, Stephen A. Douglas (hands in pockets), John J. Crittenden held back by unidentified man, Representative Lawrence M. Keitt with cane upraised and pistol behind his back, and Brooks about to hit a seated Sumner, as well as Henry Ward Beecher's declaration, "The symbol of the North is the pen; the symbol of the South is the bludgeon," from his speech at a rally in New York on May 31 after the caning, ca. 1856. American Cartoon Print Filing Series, Library of Congress Prints and Photographs Division, Washington, D.C.

ated his "Arguments of the Chivalry," later rendered as a print. John L. Magee made the most reprinted depiction in his "Southern Chivalry—Arguments against Club's." Both are from a viewpoint sympathetic to and using Henry Ward Beecher's line from his speech at the rally in the Broadway Tabernacle on May 30: "The symbol of the North is the pen; the symbol of the South is the bludgeon." Magee's construction of the scene is more vivid. Brooks is in mid-blow and crouching over Sumner's prostrate form like a panther with his arm outstretched, obscuring his features. Sumner is bleeding from his head with his writing arm holding a quill, the arm in Brooks's grip. Sumner's chair is on its side and his inkpot draining onto the floor. There are several men in the background grinning at the scene. Winslow's illustration is slightly more sedate, with Brooks about to strike the first blow, Keitt with cane in the air warding off onlookers, and Douglas and Toombs passively standing by.

The message of these two prints is crystal clear, and so is their use of

Christ-like metaphors. Behind their creation are the same demands, conceptions, and constraints of the mass media markets that the writers faced. While Winslow's print has more authenticity with its identifiable faces, the Magee image is more striking. Oddly enough, part of the reason why Brooks was in that posture was that Magee did not know what he looked like as Brooks was relatively unknown before the incident.[31] The two illustrations did their part in making more concrete what had become disputed in the media circus.

The North also had a great many public meetings and rallies in order to denounce Brooks and defend Sumner's rights, if not the man, and the North against an emboldened, violent South. The gatherings in New York and Boston were of particular note as they drew large, nonpartisan crowds. Although they failed in the first rally in Boston, the Republicans managed to draw attention away from Sumner's provocative words and give prominent moderates and conservatives the leading roles in the other gatherings. The resolutions were of no legal importance, but the speeches to the crowds of thousands, later reprinted for tens of thousands, helped crystallize northern opinion around the Republicans' chosen themes. They would become the chant at the national convention later that summer: Free Soil, Free Labor, Free Men, Free Speech, and Frémont. To a lesser extent Republicans could also link the events in Kansas—nonstarters to a degree before the assault—to Brooks's attack on Sumner. Bleeding Sumner reinforced the idea of Bleeding Kansas.

The South's rallies largely arose in a reaction to the ones in the North. The most notable gatherings were in South Carolina, upon Brooks's effort to seek reelection, not a difficult task considering that he was running unopposed (as was Keitt). The public showered Brooks with gifts of canes with such inscriptions as "Hit him again" and "Knock-down arguments."

It was not that these observations were new. Orators, writers, and activists both North and South had been making those points for some time. However, the passionate partisans had rarely gained the upper hand. Even Brooks made attempts to moderate the circus atmosphere of the rallies. His innate lack of confidence had perhaps finally bubbled to the surface. In a letter to his brother during the weeks following the assault, Brooks admitted that he was rapidly tiring of the attention: "The responsibility of my position is painfully heavy, for I have lost my individuality in my representative capacity. I am regarded to a great extent as the exponent of the South against which Black Republicanism is warring in my person."[32]

But a thing is what it is, and Brooks was now the darling of the fire-eaters. When he returned to South Carolina in the fall, his public remarks reflected this shift in his rhetorical positions. He declared at one point, "I have been a disunionist since the time I could think." This was patently not true—unless he had been lying in his previous speeches about secession being a last resort. In addition, he stated, "The Constitution of the United States should be torn to fragments and a Southern Constitution formed in which every State should be a slave state."[33] His political stance had shifted in light of events that he had influenced at least in part.

It is not surprising that Brooks had changed as a result of the assault. Those engaging in violence are affected by the conduct of it. Even if one has been trained in it, subscribed to a philosophy of violence like the honor code, and lived in a world of it, one cannot help but be affected by such an altercation. Moreover, Brooks was not left to deal with his own recollection of what he had done; he had become a celebrity. We are very familiar with the impact this status can have on a person. We live in a celebrity culture. The tales of lost privacy, feelings of isolation, and a psychology of living exposed in a fish bowl are legion. Brooks also had the burden of being hated in a majority of the country. As such the public's verdict on the assault was a mixed bag for all concerned.

The Congress, in the form of the House of Representatives, had found Brooks guilty of the assault and condemned it. But the fact that the vote had been on largely party and sectional lines made the judgment appear less than impartial. The court had also found Brooks guilty, but only of a minor infraction and with a fairly light punishment. The handling of the Brooks-Sumner affair in Congress and the court convinced many in the North that the slave power extended to the courts of law, or rather provided additional evidence of that fact. The court of public opinion, as demonstrated in the newspapers, rallies, and expressions of sympathy or support, was similarly divided. Both areas of the country reacted to the news. Both areas saw the other's reaction. Both reacted to that reaction.

The nature of the venue affected the portrayal of the assault in different ways. The two committees of the Congress reflected the political makeup of each house, as well as the rules of each. The Senate's investigation was the result of Democratic domination and its more deliberate, cautious, and judicious understandings of its own authority. The House committee and the House's actions were the result of Republican and American Party preponderance plus the House's ability to carry through with the will of its majority. Both houses were interpreting law in order to reach their respective conclusions. The issues were questions of free speech, personal liberty, and whether the House had the authority to act in such a case. They created legal records according to the rules of court-like proceedings and deliberated as a jury might based on that evidence.

Although a legal proceeding, this did not mean that the court acted out of its political, social, and cultural context. The judge and prosecutor were Democrats appointed by Democratic presidents. Their decisions reflected not just the law in the case but their own concepts of what was appropriate. These concepts stemmed from their personal understandings of the severity of the crime, which were influenced by their sympathies and self-interest. Brooks's defense targeted this soft underbelly of the law. He appealed to notions of justice present in the common law, in the community in which he stood, which also happened to share aspects of the legal culture in which he was raised, trained, and practiced as an attorney. While we cannot peer into Crawford's mind, we can interpret his decision in light of these circumstances. The outcome of the trial showed all the permutations of a democratically ordered common-law system. Despite the testimony of eyewitnesses that showed a dangerous, premeditated attack on a vulnerable victim, largely without warning, the perpetrator was held to be responsible only for a minor infraction.

Public opinion reflected as well as shaped politics, culture, and society. The newspapers' need to sell copies existed alongside their desire to reach their readership, mold opinion, and serve their notion of the republic. In the imperfect realm of knowledge that is the world of mass media, there were constraints on their ability to convey nuance, the countervailing forces within law and politics, and the hidden motives behind the primary actors in this drama. Our interpretation of the inflammatory editorials, pictorials, and sensationalist news items stems from our view of the media's purpose, as well as the outcome of this sequence of events, the Civil War. One of the nation's first mass media circuses played a critical role in magnifying and sustaining the controversy. How we view that war and the run-up to it determines our evaluation of the media's part in that story.

We do not just care about the caning's immediate impact on events. There is still a great deal of history between May 22, 1856, and April 1861 when the first shots of the Civil War resounded. The question remains whether the caning merely grabbed headlines and occupied Congress briefly or had a long-term influence on the events that followed. The most prominent domino in the sequence to fall next was the fall elections of 1856. The fates of Brooks, Sumner, Keitt, Burlingame, Edmundson, and their parties would be determined in the campaigns of that summer and fall.

4 | A LONG, WINDING ROAD

FROM MAY 22, 1856, to April 9, 1865, the question that began as why one man would strike another became why so many men went to kill one another. The immediate answer was the election of Abraham Lincoln in 1860 as president of the United States. A more complicated question then follows: why would that election cause the Deep South to secede, followed, after much political maneuvering, by much of the Upper South? Why did both sides refuse to accept the status quo and plunge the nation into civil war? Oddly enough, the answers to these questions might be the same. A series of events accrue until one American strikes another. For our purposes we might wonder whether the answers are causally related. Did the caning of Charles Sumner cause the Civil War?

The Election of 1856

The events themselves are plain enough. James Buchanan, a doughface Democrat, becomes president in 1857. A deep recession begins the month after he takes office. In a bid to placate the South, he favors the Lecompton Constitution, a proslavery document, for Kansas. The Supreme Court weighs in on the issue of slavery in *Dred Scott v. Sanford* (1857), the chief justice declaring that slavery cannot be abridged by congressional action. In any case, a majority of the Court, all Democratic politicians before they ascended the bench, finds that a slave taken into free states and territories does not retain that freedom when he is returned to slave country. The elections of 1858 follow with Abraham Lincoln's unsuccessful bid to replace Stephen Douglas as a senator from Illinois. In a series of widely publicized debates (telegraph and newspapers once again to the fore), Lincoln gains prominence for himself and forces Douglas to admit to the Freeport Doctrine. The exchange is still known and celebrated as the Lincoln-Douglas debates. Finally, John Brown raids Harpers Ferry, Virginia, in an abortive attempt at a slave insurrection, in 1859. Brown and his cohorts are captured, tried, and hanged. Like the caning of Sumner, each section's observation of the other's reaction to John Brown's execution—mourning in the North, repugnance in the South—solidifies their distrust of the other.

Under this barrage of crises, the fractured election of 1860 seems more like an afterthought. Even if the Democratic Party had been united, Lincoln would have won the election by a clear majority of electoral votes. Despite garnering only about 40 percent of the popular vote and not even appearing on the ballot, by law, in the slaveholding states, the North solidly approved the free-soil Republican platform. What motivated fire-eaters to push all but Delaware, Maryland, Kentucky, and Missouri among the slaveholding states into secession and rebellion? How could they not view Lincoln and the Republicans, although a minority in the Senate and a slight majority in the House, as a threat?

Like the answer to the question of why Brooks caned Sumner, we can only find it in a close examination of those events following the caning. There is little doubt "Bleeding Sumner" contributed to the dramatic growth in the Republican Party through the election of 1856. Its national convention, in June, took place in the shadow of the unfolding scandal. Cleverly, in addition to nominating the nonpolitical Frémont, the Republicans broadened their national platform beyond their origins as merely an anti–Kansas-Nebraska Act coalition with the addition of the Whig program of tariffs and infrastructure improvements, such as national support for railroads. This cemented conservative northern support for what one historian has called the free labor ideology. Based largely on the contrast with the slave power ideology, the free labor ideology centered on the identification of non-slaves with the survival, origins, and expansion of the republic. In this formulation, antipathy to the expansion of slavery was not just about farmland for northern transplants but about a competing worldview emphasizing liberty, economic opportunity, the rule of law, and republican government.

While the labeling of the Democrats as opponents of these values seems to exemplify party politics in the extreme, this version of the "caning of Sumner" story resonated in the North. Sumner was exercising his free speech rights. He was performing his legislative duty of speaking up for free labor and condemning the slave power. The slave power's response came in the form of a brutal, murderous, and cowardly attack. The inferior, barbaric, and lawless slavery proponent had struck down the superior, civilized, and lawful knight of liberty. In their own way, the Republicans had their own honor system. What Brooks had done violated their honor code. The criminal court's failure to punish Brooks accentuated the point.

It was not an appeal that would resonate in the slaveholding states, but the Republican Party was not seeking conciliation, compromise, and the forging of nationwide coalitions even if the electoral laws of the South had permitted it. The Republicans relied on a predominance strategy that utilized the immense advantages of the free labor states—population, productivity, and a political inferiority complex—to win control of the national government. Although many often mistake the Republicans as a sectional party, in 1860, with the admission of Minnesota and Oregon, the free states of the Union were a majority in number of states and in population. Republicans were not battling to be a majority in a section of the country; they were working for predominance in the whole of the country with the exception of the isolated slaveholding South.

The Democrats were not idle. Although the southern wing was now dominant, they still had a substantial draw in New York, Pennsylvania, and Illinois, among other places. For their candidate they settled on James Buchanan, who had been the ambassador to Britain during the Kansas-Nebraska controversy and, thus, had not been tainted with it. It was a compromise choice on the seventeenth ballot. The southern delegation had wanted Douglas or Pierce, and the northern delegation neither. As events would show, the Northerners could not have been more wrong about Buchanan.

The election of 1856 was not just between the Republicans and the Democrats. The American or Know-Nothing Party was still a force, although the slavery issue proved a substantial problem. The northern elements of the party broke apart for the second time when the southern faction managed to make Millard Fillmore the nominee. Fillmore had made several lukewarm statements on Kansas-Nebraska and been permanently discredited in the eyes of northern leaders. When the Northern Americans, as they became known, sought fusion with the Republicans, the Republican leadership, sensing victory in their contest for free-state votes, politely refused to accept the Northern Americans' nominee for the vice presidential spot, William P. Johnston. This firm stand forced the Northern Americans to accept the Republican Party nominees or nothing. The remnant of the American Party ran Fillmore to little effect.

The Democrats only needed a little effort to win the election for Buchanan. Fillmore's 14 percent of the popular vote was decisive in costing Frémont Indiana, Illinois, and Pennsylvania. If Buchanan had lost these states, the Republicans would have captured the White House a mere two years after their formation as a political party. As it stood, the Whig Party had now largely vanished as a national political organization, and while the Republicans and the American Party had lost control of the House of Representatives and were still badly outnumbered in the Senate, they were well positioned for the by-election of 1858 and the presidential contest of 1860 if they could continue to consolidate their sectional gains. They were fortunate as well that the Democrats could not hide the slavery issue.

Dred Scott v. Sanford and the "Self-Inflicted Wound"

The first boon to the Republicans during the Buchanan presidency did not come from the president, although he did have a hand in it, but from the United States Supreme Court in the form of *Dred Scott v. Sanford*. The opinions of the justices were announced on March 6, just after the presidential inauguration. Then, Buchanan made reference to the court's impending decision as the proper authority for deciding the issue of popular sovereignty. In fact, he had a hand in it. But nothing about *Dred Scott* was that simple. The only thing we know for sure is that Dred Scott lost the case and, thus, his suit for freedom by a seven-to-two vote. Oddly enough, even the name of the appellee, John Sanford, was misspelled by the clerk of the Supreme Court as Sandford. The rest of the case is mired in controversy even to this day.

Perhaps this is not so surprising given the incredibly circuitous route these ten years of litigation took to reach the nation's highest tribunal. The story began with a lawsuit Dred Scott filed in 1846. Although he was a slave, Missouri courts allowed slaves to sue for their freedom if the suit did not directly seek such a remedy. While defenders of slavery would later allege that this was an abolitionist plot, it was more likely that a friendly family in Missouri was doing what untold thousands had done before—seeking freedom for someone they knew. Scott was not just seeking his own liberation. He had a wife, Henrietta, although technically under slave law he was not allowed to legally marry, and children, although under slave law they were not his or his wife's, but belonged to his master the way that a colt or a calf belongs to the owner of the mare or the cow.

His suit alleged that his previous owner now deceased, a Dr. Emerson, had taken him into free territory and a free state, Illinois. There he met and married Henrietta. Emerson had also taken the couple into the Minnesota Territory, free under the Missouri Compromise. Scott alleged that he had been liberated as a result of his residence in these areas. His claims challenged several aspects of slavery law. First, his claim for freedom tested whether Congress could forbid slavery in a territory. Second, he tested whether slavery ended when a slave was domiciled in (not just transported through) a free state. Third, it tested the relationship between a slave state, Missouri, and free states, under the doctrine of comity.

At the time Scot first filed his suit in Missouri court, Missouri had a precedent supporting his claim, but, owing to a filing error, he had to file a second time. The delay brought the case on appeal to the Missouri State Supreme Court in the aftermath of the ill will the Compromise of 1850 had created, particularly regarding the Fugitive Slave Law. Free states were passing personal liberty laws, and slaveholding states were no longer in a giving mood. In 1852, the Missouri Supreme Court ruled that residing in a free territory and a free state did not make a slave free in Missouri. Hoping to appeal this ruling on a matter that involved an issue of federal concern, Dred Scott filed his lawsuit in federal court in 1853.

In order to fill the diversity of state citizenship requirement needed to file such a suit in federal court under the Judiciary Act of 1789, Dred Scott filed suit against the executor of Emerson's estate, John A. Sanford, a resident of New York. This created a strange legal issue for the courts. In order to file the lawsuit, Scott had to show diversity of citizenship. In order to show citizenship, he needed to be free. In order to be free, he needed to prevail in his lawsuit. It also gave the United States Supreme Court an easy out. They could simply rule a lack of diversity of citizenship and leave it at that. They could have also ruled that the procedure at issue in the appeal to the court— the plea in abatement—was not properly before the court, thus sustaining the Missouri Supreme Court's ruling. However, President-elect Buchanan, Chief Justice Roger B. Taney, and a substantial number of other justices had another purpose in mind.

By the time Dred Scott appealed the adverse lower federal court's ruling to the Supreme Court on December 30, 1854, the Kansas-Nebraska imbroglio was in full swing. The Republican Party was forming, Whigs were being buffeted into destruction, and the Democrats in the South were becoming more aggressive on the slavery expansion question. Taney and his fellow Democrats on the bench watched these events with increasing frustration. Taney's tenure as chief justice had been marked by a distancing from his predecessor John Marshall's aversion to ruling on slave cases. Marshall preferred to avoid them or decide them on narrow factual or procedural grounds. Taney was an avid white supremacist and, moreover, a judicial supremacist, that is, he favored making the U.S. Supreme Court the ultimate decider of what was law in the United States. When you combined this theory with Taney's personal views on slavery and his avid Democratic allegiance (he was Andrew Jackson's strong right arm during Jackson's second term), it produced a desperate desire to have the Court settle the slavery expansion question once and for all. Perhaps the death of his wife and his own growing infirmity played a role as well. He was an old man in a hurry.

Thus, it was no surprise when Taney read his opinion and it dismissed Scott's claim on the procedural ground that the suit lacked diversity of citizenship because it found Scott to still be a slave. But Taney did not stop there. He insisted on making two additional holdings regarding congressional powers over the territories and the nature of the U.S. Constitution with regard to slavery. He wrote that, in effect, origin, and the framers' understanding, the Constitution was a proslavery document. In order to do this, he had to mangle English common law, the history of the Constitution, and the Court's own precedents, which were ambivalent at best on slavery. His conclusion from this tortured journey was that African-Americans could never become citizens by nature, from law, or under the Constitution. Left alone, these arguments would have set off a firestorm in the North, but Taney had more to say.

Possibly goaded by the dissenters' decision from very early on to pronounce their own judgment on Congress's power over slavery in the territories, Taney made the startling argument that all of Congress's attempts to limit slavery, including the Missouri Compromise line of 1820, were unconstitutional. Despite the Constitution's explicit grant of authority over the territories to Congress in Article IV, the chief justice argued that the "takings clause" of the Fifth Amendment, when combined with the proslavery stance of the Constitution, prohibited the Congress and any state, under the Comity Clause of Article IV, from interfering with slavery. As opposed to the arguments of Justice John McLean, Sumner, and other antislavery advocates, Taney made clear that slavery was the default position in American law and protected under the Constitution.

Taney's opinion in *Dred Scott* indicates several things of importance. First, it gave many editorial writers, politicians, and other commentators further evidence of the slave power conspiracy, which included Judge Crawford, who treated Brooks so leniently. Both Crawford and Taney were Democratic appointees. Both were affiliated with or, in Taney's case, founding members of the southern wing of the party. Both were part of the Democratic- and southern-dominated capital's social scene. Both were judges of long standing.

Second, Taney felt driven to solve the problem of slavery expansion. As a true believer in the majesty of law, he based his leadership of the court on the principle of judicial conservatism and the court's supremacy as interpreter of the Constitution. As such he was a devotee of the advantages of courts and judges over legislatures and legislators. Regardless of the strong language he and dissenter Benjamin Curtis employed in their opinions, neither would dream of using the personal invective and attacks Sumner, Butler, Clay, Mason, Douglas, and their ilk used as part of their appeals. (Curtis was furious with what he perceived as Taney's slights during the deliberations and shortly thereafter resigned from the Court.)

Third, Taney was not isolated from the swirl of events around him. As late as 1828, Taney had opposed slavery, both in court and in his personal life—freeing the eight slaves he had inherited. However, the Taney of the late 1850s was in many respects a different man. Suffering from a host of ailments and having lost his beloved wife and one of his daughters to yellow fever two years before, he had become hardened, defensive, and anxious about the survival of the life he cherished. A devoted Catholic, he had raised his children Presbyterian in deference to his wife's beliefs but led a devout life in the church of his birth. His principles were as immutable as his faith.

The caning of Charles Sumner and its aftermath revealed deep rifts not even a chief justice of advanced years dedicated to the neutral principles of judging could have resolved. Although none of Taney's biographers or those writing on the *Dred Scott* case mention Brooks's assault as an influence on Taney or his court, the opinions in the majority in the case do share the desire to refute the arguments Sumner and other antislavery advocates were making regarding the laws and supreme law of the United States. Taney's opinion in particular shares the qualities of Butler's, Keitt's, and Brooks's antipathy toward the North, intense feelings about the Republicans, and evidence of a deep and abiding foreboding about the fate of their section. If we cannot conclude that the majority opinions in the *Dred Scott* case were a result of the caning of Charles Sumner, we can safely assume that they were part and parcel of the phenomenon the caning revealed and helped produce.

For the slave who had initiated this controversy, there was a bittersweet ending. He received his manumission only after a transfer of ownership to the son of his former owner Dr. Emerson. However, he did not have long to enjoy it; he died a year later. It was probably of little consolation—even had he known—that he outlasted Preston S. Brooks and Andrew P. Butler.

Whatever Happened to . . . ?

In another of those ironic coincidences surrounding the Brooks-Sumner affair, when the congressman caught cold, which developed into a lethal swelling in the throat on January 27, 1857, Brooks's attending physician was Dr. Cornelius Boyle, who had initially dressed Sumner's wounds. On May 25, 1857, Butler joined his cousin in death. In the North and the South, the newspapers devoted considerable coverage to both events, as well as daily postings on Brooks's brief ailment and his agonizing demise. As one would expect, their views varied with their sympathies.

Butler's and Brooks's deaths generated lamentations from their state and section. Brooks received the laurels of a fallen hero, taken too young from his countrymen. Butler was called a great statesman. Their editorialists conveniently forgot their frequent flashes of temper, their ungentlemanly language, and their bitter partisanship. Neither Butler nor Brooks had sought to forestall the coming cataclysm with concessions, nor treated their abolitionist opponents with anything but invective and contempt. Age does not make a statesman, nor does dying young make one a martyred hero, but for their supporters they did both. The papers in the North responded likewise only from the opposite side of the dispute. The Republican press viewed Brooks's death so soon after his single claim to fame as divine judgment. With that, they let sleeping dogs lie and rarely mentioned either Brooks or the caning again.

Sumner, in the meantime, had a very mixed year. He had defied his doctors and some of his friends' advice and returned to Boston to campaign for his friend Burlingame, who was in a very tight election race. It is likely that Burlingame's margin of victory was due to Sumner's efforts on his behalf, efforts exerted with noticeable frailty. The Massachusetts legislature, although concerned that his infirmity impaired his ability to represent Massachusetts, nevertheless overwhelmingly reelected him to his seat just as Brooks's and Keitt's constituents did for them. Once again against his doctors' advice, Sumner returned to the Senate in February of 1857 so that he could cast his vote for Massachusetts on the tariff bill that was so vital to her interests. A debilitating relapse of his symptoms in March caused him to quit his duties in search of a cure. From then until 1860, he traveled back and forth from Europe, only occasionally taking his place in the Senate.

The debate about the seriousness of his illness now took place largely in northern newspapers and among Massachusetts politicians. On the one side were those who argued that "the vacant chair" meant more than his presence ever could. In a way this was an insult. Being a symbol for a cause is rarely as praiseworthy as being an effective advocate of that cause. On the opposing side were those who openly speculated about the need for Sumner to retire so he could recover his health and, more importantly, yield the precious Senate seat to someone who would be fully effective. As his absence gained more ink than the original cause, Sumner sought a treatment that would rid him of his symptoms. He wanted no part of martyrdom as the headaches and weakness lingered on. He managed to fill his seat in Washington in time for the next round of strident debates over Kansas, this time the Lecompton Constitution controversy.

The Lecompton Fiasco

The fierce factional struggle that was the debate over the Lecompton Constitution was much the same as the one in 1856 that spurred Sumner's "Crime against Kansas" speech. Proslavery forces were still badly outnumbered and resorted to more electoral fraud, once again stuffing ballot boxes, in order to save Kansas for slavery. The Democratic presidential administration, this time under Buchanan, still tried to placate the South by supporting the proslavery portion of the territory. Southern states like Texas and Alabama were still threatening to secede if Kansas did not become a slave state. In addition, despite the *Dred Scott* case, the Congress still had to face the Kansas issue with an eye toward the elections coming the next year, 1858.

In some ways, the debate over Lecompton was different than the "Bleeding Kansas" fracas of two years before. Although the Lecompton convention had already met under the proslavery legislature, a more recent election in October 1856 had installed a free-state legislature. With a democratically elected legislature in control and territorial governors recognizing free-soil predominance, violence had largely subsided. When elections on January 4, 1857, confirmed Free-Soilers' control over state offices, the "rebellion" of the Topeka movement ended. The new government provided for a referendum to counter the partial submission referendum the Lecompton convention had ordered, which the Free-Soilers had boycotted. In that referendum, the voters of Kansas overwhelmingly rejected the Lecompton Constitution. For this reason, Stephen Douglas, reflecting his true popular sovereignty commitments and with an eye for his own reelection in 1858, opposed the Lecompton Constitution. Buchanan would spend much of 1857 campaigning against this pillar of his own party in order to get Congress to admit Kansas as a slave state.

From February 2, when Buchanan sent the Lecompton Constitution to Congress under the pretext that Kansas was "as much a slave state as Georgia or South Carolina," the Congress and newspapers warred about Kansas. In spite of Douglas's opposition, the Senate consented by a vote of 33 to 25 on March 23. The real contest came in the House. Sentiment in the free states was solidly against Lecompton. The Michigan, New Jersey, and Rhode Island legislatures passed resolutions against it. The Ohio legislature instructed Senator George Pugh to vote against it. The newspapers in the North were almost uniformly opposed.

All of this propelled Laurence Keitt into the spotlight once again. In the course of debate on Lecompton on February 4, Keitt declared to Galusha Grow of Pennsylvania, "Sir, I will let you know you are a Black Republican puppy." Grow responded, "Never Mind. No negro-driver shall crack his whip over me." With that Keitt went after Grow. Not sitting at his desk and caught unawares like Sumner, Grow flattened Keitt with a single blow to the jaw. The rest of what transpired, a truly hair-raising brawl, has already been described.[1]

On April 1, the anti-Lecompton Democrats arranged for a compromise.

They substituted Senator John J. Crittenden's proposal for a resubmission of the document to Kansas for a vote and passed it by a small majority. As a result of this disagreement between the two houses, a conference committee met. In order to resolve the impasse, the conference committee, with Buchanan's support, proposed another compromise, known as the English bill after Representative William H. English, in which Kansas's request for public land was reduced, she would receive the opportunity to vote on Lecompton again, but, if she rejected it, she would not be allowed to apply for admission as a state until her population reached ninety thousand rather than sixty thousand. Supposedly, this conditional grant allowed Southerners the face-saving ability to deny that they had agreed to resubmit Lecompton to a vote as it was a new proposal. The English bill passed both the House and Senate on April 30. When Kansans overwhelmingly rejected Lecompton again in a vote on August 2, the Kansas issue died until after the election of 1860. Kansas would be admitted as a state, but only in 1861 after the majority of the Democratic South had walked out of Congress.

Once more the nation convulsed with sectional strife, not simply among its politicians, but also among its people in their press, town meetings, and rallies. It did not begin with the reaction to the caning of Charles Sumner, but it certainly followed its trajectory and was a natural outgrowth of it. The nation was now familiar with the issues, the stands of all those involved, what was at stake, and the course of any debate. The only question that remained was what incident would start the process all over again.

Final Rounds

The Lincoln-Douglas debates from August 21 through October 15 were a different kind of incident on the road to the Civil War. These seven encounters between the two Illinois Senate candidates attained a kind of mythic status, no doubt in part because of Lincoln's ascent to the leadership of the Republican Party. Much has been made of the Freeport Doctrine—a statement Douglas made in the debate in Freeport—and its impact on Douglas's presidential campaign in 1860, but the reality was that Douglas's position within the Democratic Party was already clear, and thus his argument that slavery could be denied by a territory did not do his reputation any more irreparable damage in the South than he had already suffered. There was nothing to damage. His opposition to Lecompton had already made him anathema there.

Perhaps more important than the Freeport Doctrine or Douglas's eventual victory was the springboard the debates provided for Lincoln's rise to prominence. It was one of the great oddities in American political history that a southern-born man from a family with Virginian heritage would be the stand-in for the antislavery Republicans while a man born and bred in New England would be the representative of the Democrats. Like Brooks and Sumner, both Lincoln and Douglas were lawyers. Unlike Brooks and Sumner, they were both very good at their profession, although in different ways. Lincoln affected a country-bumpkin style that won over juries, while Douglas tended more for the small-town style that impressed business interests. This was, strangely enough, the exact opposite of where they received their strongest support, Douglas from southern and Lincoln from northern Illinois. There was also the fact that Lincoln's six-foot four-inch, lanky frame made him more of a Don Quixote to Douglas's Sancho Panza than Butler's height did over Douglas.

Nevertheless, their exchanges on slavery extension made it clear that both opposed it. Lincoln was direct in his policy stance, preferring an outright ban, while Douglas believed that slavery's natural limits would confine it to its current boundaries. Therefore, popular sovereignty could be trusted to act against slavery wherever it became an issue. Neither candidate offered the South the concessions its advocates demanded. Neither pronounced what they would have done to confront secessionist movements. It is also noteworthy that neither used the strident language of Sumner or the fire-eaters.

Lincoln's statement on the conflict came before the debates on June 16 at the state Republican convention in Springfield. It is known as his "House Divided" speech, in which he paraphrased scripture by saying "'A house divided against itself cannot stand.' I believe this government cannot endure, permanently half slave and half free."[2] How much of this was rhetoric, a prediction, or policy we cannot know. It was certainly how many both North and South felt. Lincoln spent most of the speech on the *Dred Scott* case, the Kansas-Nebraska Act, and Douglas's relation to the two. He never mentioned the caning.

William H. Seward declared his own version of the "house divided" concept in a speech subsequently known as the "Irrepressible Conflict" speech on October 25, 1858, in Rochester, New York. The basis for his conclusion was the free labor ideology. The bulk of it was a recounting of recent history. The memorable lines were as follows: "It is an irrepressible conflict between opposing and enduring forces, and it means that the United States must and will, sooner or later, become either entirely a slaveholding nation, or entirely a free-labor nation." His history was that of a slave power conspiracy. He only obliquely referred to the caning if at all when he talked about the Kansans and said the Democrats "drove them with menaces and intimidations from the halls of Congress," leaving us with the conclusion that neither Seward nor Lincoln cared to use the caning as even a talking point despite its applicability to their conflict and the clash between two different systems' claims.[3]

Why not? One possibility is that their campaigns in 1858 had moved beyond the caning to more recent, more relevant events. The caning was yesterday's news. Brooks was dead and buried, literally. Another possibility is that there was a lurid aspect to the bloody assault that they were trying to avoid. It is difficult to assert the temper to rule while engaging in visceral politics, the appeal to emotion, prejudice, and sensationalism that marks you as little more than a rabble-rouser. Finally, these were speeches given to draw attention to the speaker. Lincoln was beginning his campaign for Douglas's Senate seat. Seward was aiding his party in New York with an eye on the Republican nomination for president in 1860. It was not particularly useful to mention another prominent Republican, particularly since the martyrdom aspect was now being replaced by a debate over whether Sumner should resign. Although these speeches latently repeated the caning story in the form of the evils of the slave power, the fight over slavery extension, and the conflict with the South, the caning incident itself was absent.

Another stalking horse in the election of 1858 was the economy. Since the recession of 1854, the United States had undergone a significant expansion in overall production, construction, and the financial speculation that went along with it. However, the preconditions of this prosperity began to evaporate beginning in 1856 with the end of the Crimean War. Like all wars in Europe that created a grain shortage, this one had been very profitable for American farmers. But all good things must come to an end, and when the Russian government signed a peace treaty with their opponents Britain, France, and the Ottoman Empire, the demand for American exports declined. If this were not enough, the French government of Napoleon III had borrowed heavily from British investors in order to finance their participation in the war. These investors responded to the close of hostilities by selling their American securities for safer British ones as France threatened to default. This in turn caused a run on New York financial markets. All the highly leveraged American economy needed was an incident to set off a financial panic that would cause a bust. It came in the form of the collapse of the Ohio Life Insurance and Trust Company, a bank (despite its name) in New York City.

From August 24, 1857, when the Ohio Life Insurance and Trust Company announced its failure, until December 1857, when the panic subsided, the suspension of bank payments, bank failures, and runs on banks rippled throughout the economy, causing factories to shut down, construction to grind to a halt, and unemployment to overload the charities that were the only source of aid for those out of work. Without a national bank to provide liquidity to the system or rein in the reckless speculation that was its source, government could do little to stem the recession. Cutting taxes and deficit spending on public works were not even a twinkle in anyone's eye, the former because there were no income taxes to cut and the latter because Keynesian deficit spending to revive an economy was seventy years in the future, even as a theory. People responded in much the same way as they had since at least the days of Hamilton and Jefferson: they turned to politics.

The Republicans took the opportunity to publicize their adoption of the Whig program for infrastructure improvements, the homestead proposal in which small lots would be sold to homesteaders at low rates, and a higher tariff to protect domestic manufacturing. Behind it all was the commitment to the free labor ideology. By contrast, southern Democrats used the economic downturn as an example of why the free labor system could not compete with that of the slaveholding South. At the same time, they sought new lands for slavery so they could grow the slave trade market and rescue their economy from the recession. Northern Democrats were caught in the middle.

The result of the elections for the Thirty-sixth Congress in 1858 came as no surprise considering the twin disasters that were the Lecompton debate and the recession. The Democrats lost their majority in the House in devastating fashion, going from 132 seats to 83. The Republicans went from 90 to 116, three short of an outright majority, which they made up for by forging coalitions with either the American Party remnant or the anti-Lecompton Democrats in the North. The Democrats retained their majority in the Senate, but the Republicans gained six seats, a threatening trend should additional states like Kansas gain admission to the Union.

With this divided government, it was unlikely that either of the major parties would be able to enact their legislative agendas. Nevertheless, Northerners managed to agree on two substantial pieces of legislation: a homestead bill and a bill for land grant colleges. The bill for land grant colleges came from Vermont Republican Justin S. Morrill, who had picked up the idea from two substantial movements: the education reform movement and the agricultural reform movement, which both stemmed from largely Federalist sources. Later taken up by incipient professional organizations for teachers and scientific agriculturalists, these two groups worked in tandem to support a program for federal funding of colleges for the mechanical and agricultural arts through federal land sales. In spite of largely southern opposition based on states' rights and anti–large government ideas, the House and Senate passed both bills.

Southerners took at least two lessons from these votes. First, they were now isolated ideologically as well as politically in their defense of the slave system. The majority of the country was now in the hands of a free labor ideology, or at least more susceptible to it. The second conclusion came from the fact that only James Buchanan's veto of both bills stood between them and that agenda's enactment. If the Republicans could gain control of the presidency, only a Democratic Senate would place a hindrance on Republican domination of the national government. An event in 1859 brought home the importance of this trajectory.

John Brown's Body

John Brown had suffered many failures in his life. His financial enterprises had all failed. His desire to lead a life of moral purity had fallen well short of his goals. He had lied to creditors, courts, and his community in the course of those derelictions. In some respects, he was even a failure as a father and leader of the cause that dominated the final decade of his life—abolitionism. But, oddly enough, in failure John Brown did manage to advance his cause.

He had led the raid in Kansas that became known as the Pottawatomie Massacre for its brutal murdering of five proslavery settlers the night of May 24 and the morning of May 25, 1856. He succeeded only in bringing down the wrath of the national and territorial governments on the free-state majority. A guerilla war lasting the rest of the summer and solving little was the result. His motive for leading four of his sons and their fellows on this house-to-house set of murders with swords, knives, and rifles was to bring to the proslavery forces the violence they had inflicted on others.

According to recollections significantly after the fact, besides the "Sack of Lawrence" three days before, one of the instigating events had also been the news of Preston S. Brooks's attack on Charles Sumner. "At that blow the men went crazy—*crazy*. It seemed to be the finishing, decisive touch," Jason Brown, one of John Brown's sons, recalled.[4] The truth about the massacre would be overshadowed by the publicity Brown received in his unsuccessful defense of Osawatomie, but his die was cast as the violent abolitionist. Whatever its immediate impact had been, the caning's violence continued to influence John Brown's next significant venture.

On the evening of October 16, 1859, with the weapons and supplies he had raised from sympathetic abolitionists in the North, John Brown and twenty-one other men, including three of his sons, crossed into Virginia from Maryland. Their target was the federal arsenal with its one hundred thousand guns in Harpers Ferry, Virginia, at the confluence of the Shenandoah and Potomac Rivers. Their plan was to seize the arsenal and use the large store of weapons and ammunition there to arm the slaves of Virginia in a massive insurrection. Although they were able to overwhelm the one guard easily, word of the operation carried swiftly to the militias and federal troops in the area. By October 18, a group of marines under the command of Lieutenant Colonel Robert E. Lee, Mexican-American War hero and future commander of the Confederacy's Army of Northern Virginia, surrounded Brown and the remainder of his party in a brick building. When Brown refused to surrender to Lee's lieutenant, J. E. B. Stuart, who would also be a general in the Army of Northern Virginia, the marines stormed the building, captured Brown, and protected their prisoners from the lynch mob that had gathered outside.

Brown's trial lasted one week, and the jury deliberated for three-quarters of an hour before delivering their verdict on November 2: guilty of murder, treason against the state of Virginia, and inciting a slave insurrection. On December 2 before fifteen hundred soldiers and a young actor named John Wilkes Booth, who had infiltrated the proceedings in a borrowed uniform, Brown was hanged. He was fifty-nine.

Brown had become the most polarizing person in the country. In between his border crossing and his execution, his letters and interviews with reporters had made national news. Republicans were nearly unanimous in condemning the raid as a folly at best. They were anxiously trying to avoid association with what was plainly an illegal, radical, and ill-conceived enterprise. After all, the vast majority of Republicans were not abolitionists, much less the violent, fanatical abolitionist of Brown's sort. Some in the North did praise him. Henry David Thoreau wrote, "Some eighteen hundred years ago Christ was crucified; this morning, perchance, Captain Brown was hung. These are the two ends of a chain which is not without its links. He is not Old Brown any longer; he is an angel of light."[5] Reflecting the martyrdom of John Brown among many communities in the North, church bells tolled on the news of his execution, black bunting adorned many a house, memorial gatherings were held, encomia in newspapers and hastily printed books and lithographs flowed in their thousands, and visitors to his grave in North Elba, New York, made it look like a national shrine.

As with the caning of Charles Sumner, John Brown's raid, trial, and execution were viewed differently in the South. Virginia and other border states heightened their patrols. Believing that Brown's raid must have been part of a larger plot, their congressmen investigated and their press fulminated against the vile abolitionists who supposedly ran the North. In observing the reaction of some in the North, many in the South became convinced of northern hostility, not simply toward slavery's expansion but toward its very existence. Robert Toombs spoke for many when he implored on the Senate floor, "Never permit this Federal government to pass into the traitorous hands of the black Republican party."[6] Open sentiments of secession were now not just the province of fire-eaters in South Carolina but expressed in most of the major newspapers and by most of the congressmen throughout the slaveholding South.

Some historians and contemporaries questioned John Brown's sanity, and they took much the same view of Sumner for the same reasons. More recent histories have noted that Brown's supposed insanity took the form of a desperate attempt to liberate African-Americans from slavery against terrible odds, including the innate conservatism of the Republican Party. His passionate commitment to his cause was no less than Sumner's, and its opponents and subsequent scholars condemned their actions because Sumner and Brown fomented the war their critics thought they should have tried to avoid. A key difference was that John Brown's mettle, rectitude, and stoicism impressed even the Virginians he had terrorized. Sumner received no such plaudits in his anguished recovery. What we cannot doubt is that both events created and reflected circumstances of deep emotions about slavery, union, and what constituted the law of the land. It was against this background that the elections of 1860 took place.

The Election of 1860 and the Secession Movement

Aiding the Republicans in their cause was a disaffected writer from North Carolina's Piedmont region. Hinton Rowan Helper had some success as a negative publicist with his volume ridiculing the myths behind California's gold rush, *The Land of Gold*, in 1854. In 1857, he turned his bitter pen to the issues raised in the 1850 census. The result was a book, *The Impending Crisis of the South: How to Meet It*, offering a vast array of statistics to prove what many in the South already sensed—that the South was falling dreadfully behind the growing, industrializing North. Helper went further: he blamed the South's supposed retardation on slavery. He advocated abolition, repatriation of all African-Americans, and a poor white alliance to do so.

Helper was not an abolitionist because he believed in equality among races. To the contrary, he was an unabashed bigot. His anger and arguments stemmed from pride in his region and race and a hatred of slavery that, he believed, hurt them both. He had to publish his book in and relocate to New York City because it was against the law to openly advocate abolition in speech or publication in the slaveholding South. Thus, among abolitionists and some Republicans, Helper became a propagandist advocate not for his own region but among the voters of the North. With help from wealthy donors, the Republicans printed several thousand copies of a campaign version of the book, *Compendium of the Impending Crisis of the South*, with the more incendiary racism excised. Although its impact on the election is not certain, southern politicians were incensed enough about it for John S. Millson of Virginia to declare during the contested speaker election of 1859 that "one who consciously, deliberately, and of purpose lent his name and influence to the propagation of such writings is not only not fit to be speaker, but is not fit to live."[7] Millson was no junior congressman. He was a fifty-one-year-old five-term representative by that point. Helper had hit a nerve.

Presaging what was to come, once more, the House had devolved into a contested arena rather than a deliberative lawmaking body. Tensions were so high that members were once again arming themselves. During one heated moment, a New York congressman let his pistol drop, setting off a scramble to determine the extent of the threat. Senator Hammond reported, possibly jokingly, that "The only persons who do not have a revolver and a knife are those who have two revolvers." The ground was ripe for fire-eaters like Keitt to declare in open debate that he was ready to "shatter this Republic from turret to foundation stone."[8] The election calendar played a role in this debacle. With only the December and the next year's session before the November contest for the presidency, there was little time for anything except preparing campaign speeches.

It is remarkable how poorly Democrats mobilized to retain the White House. The predictable division between the less numerous, but more important, northern part of the party and the more numerous, but less important, southern part took the form of those for Stephen Douglas and those who would not accept him. It is impossible to guess at Douglas's chances of winning the election if he had had a compliant southern wing not making trouble for him. Could Douglas have won key states in the North with a no-conflict-with-the-South campaign? We do not know. What we do know is that the South did not give him a chance.

In part this was a result of location. The first meeting of the Democrats in convention began on April 23 in Charleston, South Carolina, the home of the fire-eaters. For ten days they quarreled over parliamentary matters and in fifty-nine ballots tried unsuccessfully to decide who would be the party's nominee for president. Considering that every state in the Union except South Carolina had a winner-take-all policy with winner defined as most votes, they needed to select someone who could win some of the states in the North if they wanted to win. By 1860, the free states had an outright majority, with incredibly large state delegations like New York's thirty-five, Pennsylvania's twenty-seven, and Ohio's twenty-three electoral votes, enough to swing the election to one side or the other. However, the stances of the respective sides of the Democratic Party and the rules they had adopted to keep the peace worked against such a compromise.

Owing to the fact that the convention awarded delegates based on population and not representatives in Congress, Douglas had a working majority at the convention. However, the two-thirds rule the South had imposed to block Van Buren now blocked Douglas. Despite Douglas's appeals for conceding to his nomination based on his concessions to Pierce and Buchanan and the need for unity to win the general election, the Deep South refused any compromise on a federal slave code or Douglas himself. In a caucus five days before the Charleston convention, the Alabama, Arkansas, Florida, Georgia,

Louisiana, Mississippi, and Texas delegations agreed to bolt the convention if Douglas became the nominee.

Regardless, the convention broke apart after ten days on the question of slavery in the territories. When the Douglas supporters successfully defeated a southern motion to require that slavery be protected in the territories, the Lower South delegates walked out of the convention. Even with their absence, Douglas still failed to obtain a two-thirds majority. The party agreed to reconvene in Baltimore on June 18. The deserters convened in Richmond on June 11 but could not agree on an alternative to Douglas.

In the interim, Douglas supporters managed to arrange for their own delegates to replace those of the Lower South. As a result, the convention in Baltimore became largely about whether to admit the Douglas delegations or the returning walk-outs. By majority vote Douglas had his way. Eventually, through these maneuvers the Little Giant achieved his ultimate goal, but it proved to be an empty victory. His rivals met in their own convention in Baltimore and nominated their own candidate, Buchanan's vice president John C. Breckinridge, on a proslavery platform.

Adding to the confusion, but unlikely to affect the result, was the stepchild of the old Whig Party, led by conservatives John J. Crittenden and Edward Everett from Massachusetts. They gathered on May 8 in Baltimore at their own convention. Unified in their desire to avoid strife by avoiding taking sides except on the preservation of the Union, they nominated John C. Bell of Tennessee for president and adopted a platform in support of the U.S. Constitution. This Constitutional Union Party might have been of considerable effect if organized in an earlier period of American politics, but the lines had been drawn too sharply for a compromise that contained little except vague promises.

The impetus for victory rested with the one party that could win a majority in the majority of the country (i.e., the free states)—the Republican Party. It needed a nominee who could capture both moderate and conservative votes. The so-called radical wing, which favored African-American equality and abolition, would have damaged the party's chances of appealing to the large majority of Northerners whose racism abhorred such ideas. A man like Sumner may have been useful as a rallying cry when bludgeoned into a martyr but was less so as a standard bearer for a national party seeking widespread appeal.

Both William H. Seward and Abraham Lincoln made speeches prior to the convention widely interpreted as attempts to appear more conservative for the swing voters in Illinois, Indiana, Pennsylvania, and New York. Lincoln's February 27 address at the Cooper Institute, now Cooper Union, in New York City, has become the more notable of the two. It was largely a response to Douglas's assertion that the framers of the Constitution and the document itself supported a popular sovereignty position. Ably written, it did not mention the caning but devoted some space to trying to debunk the definitiveness of the *Dred Scott* case. Whether he realized it or not, Lincoln was using many of the same arguments Sumner and others had used in their speeches and writings, but he also made sure to state, "Wrong as we think slavery is, we can yet afford to let it alone where it is, because that much is due to the necessity arising from its actual presence in the nation."[9] There would be no slavery extension, federal slave codes, or respect for *Dred Scott* in a Lincoln administration, but he would not interfere with slavery where it already existed.

From May 16 to 18, the Republicans gathered in a building called the Wigwam specially built for the convention in Chicago, Illinois. Unlike in 1856, they did not have to deal with the American Party—only with the need to attain the most votes in the free states. Their platform was an amalgam of the Whig program of internal improvements and a tariff plus the anti-slavery-extension commitments of the Free-Soilers. On the third ballot, owing to the maneuvering of adroit supporters such as David Davis, Lincoln beat Seward for the party nomination. Lincoln now led an antislavery party against the divided Democrats of Douglas and Breckinridge and the Constitutional-Unionists of Bell.

The result of the election was a clear majority of 180 electoral votes for Lincoln, although he gained only 39 percent of the total popular vote. Historians make much of the fact that Lincoln did not win a single vote in any slaveholding state outside of Maryland, Kentucky, and Missouri. Most also declare this to be the first time a sectional party won a national election. However, Lincoln did not just win in the North or in a minority of states. He won in both California and Oregon, as well as in Iowa, and would have won quite easily in Kansas had she gained admission before the election. He won seventeen states, plus a majority of New Jersey, to his opponents' fifteen states.

Moreover, we do not know if Lincoln would have gotten any of the votes in the slave states other than Virginia because he and the Republicans not only were forbidden from campaigning there but were not allowed on the ballot. Most of the slaveholding South did not tolerate freedom of debate, speech, or politics because certain topics, particularly anything that would tend to undermine slavery, were considered too dangerous even to discuss. For the same reason that slaves were illiterate by law (teaching a slave to read and write was a crime), these electoral laws were not aimed at quelling slave insurrections. They were intended to stifle the dissent of the majority of whites in the South who did not own slaves. Men like Preston S. Brooks and Laurence M. Keitt did not grow up in a land of political freedom. Questioning the existence of slavery was regarded as treason.

Regardless of these matters, the Deep South did not wait for Lincoln's inauguration to fulfill its threat to secede. Although the Republican dismissals of these threats during the campaign may be attributed to their desire to nullify the issue in the minds of free-state voters, the outright pledges of these southern state delegations, their representatives in Congress, and their newspaper editorial writers were ones the honor culture commanded they fulfill, just as Brooks felt compelled to answer Sumner.

That they would answer violently to a perceived threat rather than an actual one by seizing federal facilities and, ultimately, firing on Fort Sumter in Charleston harbor was also dictated by the same circumstances as those that motivated Brooks. The steady march of South Carolina and then Mississippi, Florida, Alabama, Georgia, Louisiana, and Texas from December 20 to February 1 out of the Union with the adoption of secession resolutions should not mislead us into thinking it was automatic. It was not. It was the result of maneuvers by fire-eaters like Keitt that may well have misrepresented the majority view.

Virginia, Arkansas, Tennessee, and North Carolina belatedly joined the Confederacy following Lincoln's call for volunteers to suppress the rebellion and the Republicans' rejection of Crittenden's compromise proposal. Crittenden had made a call for amendments to the Constitution protecting slavery and allowing its expansion south of a new compromise line. Still, neither side was eager for war. Both hoped for a relatively peaceful reconciliation. The secessionists wanted a nonviolent accession to their dissolution of their bonds, largely what Buchanan gave them during the last few, critical months of his presidency. The Republicans believed that a majority of the Confederate states' population was sympathetic to the Union and was only misled into rebellion. It was a mistaken view costly to both sides.

For the Confederacy's part, their reasoning—the same as that of Brooks when he caned the much larger Sumner—brought the states of the Confederacy into a seemingly unwinnable war. Leaving aside the border states and the more than three hundred thousand Southerners who would fight for the Union, the free states alone had a three-to-two advantage in population and possessed twice as much railroad track mileage; three times the bank deposits; 90 percent of the shoe and boot production; over 90 percent of the clothing, pig iron, firearms, and ship production; and some 60 percent of the nation's agricultural output. The leaders of the South recognized, at least in a general way, this disparity of material and human wherewithal. Like Brooks, however, the South determined that its will and its honor were the same, that an affront to honor would so magnify will that the South could not lose the war, just as Brooks knew that he would triumph in the end.

Just as Brooks had justified himself in terms of the revolutionaries' victory over a stronger foe, the leaders of the Confederacy also called history to their aid in this mystical reading of will, honor, and strength. Did the American revolutionaries, many of whom were their ancestors, not face even greater odds and triumph? Did they not face a similar choice between yielding to the great might of imperial, commercial, and more-populated Britain and resistance? Like the patriots of 1776, they anticipated help from Europe in the form of the traditional enemies of their enemies. Like the patriots of 1776, they expected to band together in a confederation and print money to finance their war. Had not the newly independent states emerged from that period of struggle some fourscore years ago even better off than they were under the empire?

Over the next four years, the Union and the Confederacy dedicated themselves to the costliest war in U.S. history. While enthusiasm for the war was consistently higher in the Confederacy until the latter stages of the conflict, both sides sacrificed enormously in order to achieve victory. The Union expended nearly 2.3 billion dollars on its effort. If one calculates the present-day value of this sum in relationship to its share of the gross domestic product—the sum of the value of all goods and services produced in the country in a year—at the time, it comes to nearly 3.5 trillion dollars. By some estimates, the material cost of the war equaled the sum total of all national government expenditures from 1787 to 1860 combined.

The Confederacy's expenditure is much more difficult to determine because, rather than raising it largely from loans and taxes, it acquired money through a liberal use of the printing press. The catastrophic inflation that resulted wiped out much of the value of the financial holdings of the Confederates. With inflation rates in the thousands of percent, Confederates took to printing counterfeit U.S. dollars in order to engage in anything besides a barter transaction. Some scholars argue that the Confederate government actually went further than the Union government in its creation of a powerful, centralized bureaucracy to manage its war effort. It is not hard to understand why. While the Confederacy had a surplus of manpower to fill its ranks in the beginning, they lacked everything else, including food, basic supplies, infrastructure, manufacturing facilities, and, much underappreciated, a financial base to wage what some scholars have termed the first modern war.

The human toll was even more staggering. U.S. forces would lose over three hundred and fifty thousand men to wounds, and the large majority to disease. When added to Confederate losses, the U.S. lost over six hundred thousand men in the Civil War. Although their losses were fewer in overall numbers, the Confederate states lost one in four white males. One of them was Laurence M. Keitt, who died at the rank of brigadier general as the result of wounds suffered in the Battle of Cold Harbor, Virginia, on June 4, 1864. Although all the families and communities who lost loved ones suffered, the states of the Confederacy were horribly devastated by the loss of many of their best and brightest, young and old, who left behind a lost generation.

The economic destruction was equally vast and concentrated in the Confederacy. Both Union and Confederate forces destroyed as they plundered the countryside for food and supplies. Much of the time the Union commissariat would leave behind IOUs, but the Confederates could not afford such niceties. Combined with the eventual Union policy most associated with General William T. Sherman's March to the Sea in 1864–65, creating a swath of devastation in order to bring home the pain of war to the civilian population, the Confederate practice of setting fire to arsenals, factories, and supplies to deny them to the enemy left much of the Confederate states' towns and cities cratered ruins. The states of the former Confederacy would not return to their prewar levels of wealth until late in the century.

The Union they failed to leave was transformed in many ways from the one that existed before the war. With the departure of the Confederate states' congressional delegations, Republicans enjoyed substantial majorities in both houses of Congress. It was something they would not have had otherwise. Now they could not only pass the Homestead and Land Grant College

(Morrill) Acts but also create a Department of Agriculture, a national banking system, a national currency, and, to help fund the war, the nation's first income tax. They raised the tariff and gave huge tracts of land to provide for the transcontinental railroad. Ultimately over two million men served in the Union army. These veterans then played a substantial role in American politics as part of the lobbying and community organization called the Grand Army of the Republic. As a result of their efforts, the U.S. government created its first version of the welfare state in the form of veterans' benefits, hospitals, and old-age homes.

Sumner's Twilight

One other issue greatly affected the country economically, socially, and politically. By the conclusion of the conflict, the Lincoln administration had shifted its policies from one of hostility toward the liberation of slaves to one of outright abolition, first in the areas still in rebellion per the Emancipation Proclamation in January 1863, then total abolition through the adoption of the Thirteenth Amendment to the Constitution on December 6, 1865. In one of the greatest ironies in American history, the states of the Confederacy brought about the exact opposite result—the extinction of slavery—than they tried to achieve by their rebellion. Through his own martyrdom and the course of events following it, Charles Sumner did see the fulfillment of one of the key objectives of his political life. His involvement in its fruition was limited to mere advocacy with Lincoln and the Congress, but he had contributed in other ways to the Union victory that made it possible.

With his travels and contacts in Europe, Sumner, now in Washington on a regular basis, helped the Union war effort with the critical area of foreign relations during the war as chair of the Senate Committee on Foreign Relations. He faced a difficult diplomatic situation. The Confederacy was using its domination of cotton production as a weapon. At the start of hostilities they stopped exporting their key crop. The result was a near shutdown of the textile industry in Europe. The Confederates were hoping that this economic stress would produce diplomatic support for or at least covert aid to their cause.

It was not a vain ambition. Many in Britain, France, and Austria were sympathetic to the secessionists. A divided United States might have served their interests very well. While Lincoln and Sumner's adroit foreign policy managed to avoid the doomsday scenario of foreign recognition for the Confederacy and the wider war that would follow, the Confederacy's ability to procure ships that raided Union commerce created enormous friction between the United States and Britain. Sumner contributed immensely to the calming of the voices in Congress, which would have brought the United States into a broader war.

Sumner was also instrumental in initiating the effort to provide for freed slaves, which became the Bureau of Refugees, Freedmen, and Abandoned Lands, known as the Freedmen's Bureau. Although the Congress rejected his plan to put it in the Treasury Department and allocate millions of acres for it to distribute to the freed slaves of the South, he contributed greatly to the effort. Unfortunately, the accession to the presidency of Andrew Johnson, a southern Democrat, upon the assassination of Abraham Lincoln on April 14, 1865, just five days after Lee's surrender at Appomattox Courthouse, ended any grand plans for the reconstruction to follow the war.

Sumner was weeping at Lincoln's bedside when the sixteenth president took his last breath. It was the beginning of the second greatest struggle of Sumner's career. He had survived the caning. He had outlived all his assailants and great rivals from 1856. However, Sumner played a very small role in the so-called Radical Reconstruction measures that sought to remake the country on the basis of African-American equality. The Fourteenth and Fifteenth Amendments, the Civil Rights Act of 1866, the Enforcement Acts of 1870 and 1871, a third Enforcement Act, also known as the Ku Klux Klan Act of 1871, and the Reconstruction Acts that set up military districts were the works of other minds, most notably Senator Lyman Trumbull of Illinois.

Sumner's one great legislative accomplishment only became law after his death, in the form of the Civil Rights Act of 1875, a memorial in many respects for the congressmen's newly departed colleague. It was a broad commitment to nondiscrimination for men whatever their "nativity, race, color, or persuasion, religious or political" in public places or accommodations. Its provisions allowed for private lawsuits and provided monetary penalties for violations or criminal prosecution for a misdemeanor. Finally, it forbade discrimination in petit or grand jury selection.[10] This basic affirmation of, protection for, and provision for a color-blind society, at least among men, lasted only until 1883 when the U.S. Supreme Court, in an opinion by Justice Joseph Bradley, declared the public facilities portions of the act an unconstitutional congressional intrusion into private matters in the *Civil Rights Cases*.[11]

Ninety years after his death, the United States made a more effective effort to embrace Sumner's dying wish of a nation committed to the equality of all its inhabitants. It took African-American service in two world wars, Nazi Germany's taking of Jim Crow laws to a genocidal level, the mass migration of African-Americans out of the South, decades of lawsuits and political struggle and protest, and a complete realignment of the two political parties that emerged from the crisis of the 1850s. A coalition of Democrats and Republicans led by a southern president, Lyndon Baines Johnson, against the Democrats of the South succeeded in framing the Civil Rights Act of 1964. A Supreme Court of both Republican and Democratic nominees insured its constitutionality in the *Heart of Atlanta Motel* decision, finding the antidiscrimination public accommodations portions of the 1964 Civil Rights Act to be constitutional.[12]

So ends the story of the caning of Charles Sumner. An assault on the floor of the U.S. Senate had electrified the nation, if only briefly. The cascade of political events that followed led to a war of such terrible destruction, cost, and sacrifice that it helped remake that nation. One hundred and fifty-two years following the caning, the political party of the man so insulted by and disgusted with an advocate of abolition that he undertook to thrash him nominated an African-American for president of the United States and gained his election.

5 ⟩ HONOR, IDEALISM, AND INEVITABILITY

IF WE view history as a stream through which almost countless events flow, what can be the significance of any one of them? We can only concern ourselves with the impact, influence, or effect of any event on those that follow. Thus, what effect did the bloody caning of Sumner have on the political crisis that soon overtook the nation? It is not an easy question to answer, because so many episodes pitting North against South, Republicans against Democrats, Free-Soilers against proslavery forces intervened between the summer of 1856 and the fateful spring of 1861.

One way to approach the question, isolating the caning from other events, would be to ask what would have happened had Brooks not beaten Sumner. Historians and lawyers occasionally ask "what if" questions (known as counterfactuals). If you remove something from a chain of events, does the outcome change? If the defendants in a lawsuit can be held responsible for the immediate effect of their actions, they bear responsibility for the resulting injury. Yet, knocking over the first in a line of dominoes does not make a person liable for their having tumbled down unless one could have foreseen the outcome of putting those dominoes in motion and deliberately did so. For our purposes, the question of significance then becomes, what would have happened differently absent the caning?

Preston S. Brooks and Charles Sumner exercised free will. Sumner need not have directed remarks at Butler, and Brooks need not have retaliated. Remember, however, that they, as well as what they thought, said, and did, were products of their very distinct societies. Considering the stormy politics of the day, when politics provided Americans their chief entertainment, Brooks and Sumner would have had a hard time avoiding some kind of conflict or at least being swept up in the conflict of section versus section and party versus party. The debate over slavery involved questions about not only law and society but also war, personalities, intrastate squabbles, the impact of mass communications, and important developments like westward expansion so encompassing that no one escaped the debate.

The reaction to the caning took place in three main areas: Congress, the courts, and the public sphere of gatherings and newspapers. Each demonstrated differences within regions, as well as critical differences between North and South. The America of 1856—whether it be the capital city, the North, the South, or the West—was a world buffeted by new trends and ideas, with older ideas still exerting their influence in powerful ways. An event as minute as an assault could become a national news item far more easily than even ten years before. The reverberations of the caning spread through the recurring election cycle even though no one mentioned it. Abraham Lincoln supposedly remarked on meeting Harriet Beecher Stowe, author of *Uncle Tom's Cabin*, "So you're the little woman who wrote the book that started this Great War!" He might well have said the same thing to Brooks, had he lived, about his caning of Charles Sumner.

One can see how difficult it is to net an event from such a swiftly flowing stream of history. But surely the election of 1856 would have unfolded quite differently without the media sensation that the caning created. Would the Republicans have emerged as a legitimate national party in the free states without it? Not likely. What was the power of "the empty chair"? Certainly, Sumner's martyrdom played a considerable role in his own reelection along with that of Anson Burlingame and other similarly situated Republicans. John Brown and the Pottawatomie Rifles also took it quite seriously if we can believe the later testimony. Without Sumner's bloody body in 1856, would the Republicans have benefited as much as they did from Lecompton, the recession of 1857, or even the red-hot southern reaction to Brown's raid on Harpers Ferry? No. The caning seems to have been a critical early domino in the falling pieces that led to the Civil War.

Still, with so many dominos crashing to the ground, so many clashes between the North and the South over slavery between 1856 and 1861, who can declare with certainty that, without the caning, some other clash between North and South would not have polarized northern and southern opinion? Members of Congress were readily issuing one another challenges, carrying arms to the Capitol, and on occasion fighting with one another on the floor of the House before the caning as well as after. Did Brooks's attack cool the tempers of other would-be combatants? Nothing in the record suggests so. In fact, the attack seems to have enflamed rather than cooled passions. Had Brooks not caned Sumner, might other warriors have turned the Capitol into a fighting arena? No two men were as unalike as they, or more suited to the uneven combat of fiery words and furious assault. Indeed, they figuratively and literally embodied differences between North and South so heated, so fervent, and so great as to constitute, in Seward's later words and Lincoln's thinking, "an irrepressible conflict."

Answers to any hypothetical questions grow out of the events that followed the Sumner-Brooks affair. If we suppose that the war was avoidable, then avoiding it becomes a moral imperative. Most people agree that wars are bad, leading as they do to death, destruction of property, and nonrecoverable expenditure. Then again, almost all of us agree that some wars are moral and we should wage them. When the Civil War came, both sides believed it necessary to fight and also that God was on their side because their cause was just. How the war evolved—the catastrophic and unnecessary loss of life from dated battlefield tactics and inadequate sanitation—stands apart from whether it should have been fought.

If indeed the war was avoidable, then the caning of Sumner looms large. It was not a necessary or sufficient cause of the war, but it certainly played a critical role. Without it, the Democrats might have maintained their control of Congress and the presidency. If the war was unavoidable, then every incendiary event carried a "flame," including the caning. It excited politics for a time, reflecting the ease with which uncontrolled passion could transform unconstrained political strife.

This short excursion through the subject of causation leads to a renewed awareness of how human choices affect history. The dispute over slavery in the western territories and the resulting election of Abraham Lincoln convinced the leadership of one section of the country to dissolve their ties with the Union. At that point, the Confederacy's leadership decided to commit the act that was the immediate or proximate cause of the conflict: the firing on Fort Sumter. Lincoln did not seek or choose a struggle of arms with the Confederates. Just because he did not shrink from it does not make him responsible for it.

Thus, the true significance of the caning lies in its vivid portrayal of the animosity between antislavery and proslavery expansionists in 1856. More specifically, the caning illustrated three very important points. First, the rule of law—the concept of "a nation of laws, not of men," the protections of the Constitution, and respect for the courts—carried little or no weight when it came to the caning. Brooks's knowledge of and respect for the law did not prevent him, a lawyer, from assaulting Sumner, another lawyer, on the floor of one of the chambers that fashioned law. The courts in Washington, D.C., did not impose anything near the full force of a legal punishment on Brooks after he admitted that the assault was intentional. Something outweighed law for Brooks. He called it honor, and nothing more clearly than the caning demonstrated that honor and lawlessness could overlap.

For his part, Sumner also regarded settled law as "immoral." He envisioned a law higher than the statutes that empowered slavery and the Constitution that permitted it. He counseled disobedience to immoral law. His dismissal of law grew out of his ideals—the great principles of liberty and equality. As such Sumner was an idealist who admitted no compromise in contravention of his values.

From their shared background as lawyers, both men knew the professional courtesies one extended not only to judge and jury but also to opponents in the adversarial or trial system. However, neither of them saw the debates over slavery extension, the meaning of the constitutional compact, and the bonds between Americans as legal matters to be argued in the courts. When Sumner spoke disparagingly of defenders of slavery and Brooks took a cane to Sumner, both men attacked the law and its adversarial system as well as each other.

Second, the caning demonstrated that slavery and slavery extension left little to no room for compromise. Even moderate Republican Abraham Lincoln made it plain in his Cooper Institute (later Cooper Union) address and his first inaugural address that, although the Constitution protected slavery where it existed and that he would not interfere with it, he considered it likely that slavery would die a natural death without additional lands. That free labor would inevitably triumph because it was a better system comprised not merely a platform plank but a pillar of every Republican's belief system. Accommodating slavery did not even enter into the equation.

The Brooks-Sumner affair brought this contest of irreconcilables into sharp relief. The old bandages could not constrain the passions behind the division, the passions that drove politicians to violence. As Lincoln conceded at the outset of his bid for the Illinois Senate seat in 1858, a house divided against itself ultimately could not stand.

When one turns to the role of Congress in the caning, one again sees how the caning prefigured and paralleled the breakup of the Union. As the branch of the federal government most likely to forge a compromise, Congress by the late 1850s found itself the least able to subdue the slavery debate. It was a small miracle that its leadership had kept the peace up to that point. Anyone could read the caning as an ill omen. If Congress could not restrain violence within its own halls, how could it restrain the violent impulses sweeping the nation? Riven by section and party, Congress became imbued with a fervor unlikely to quiet any basic political disagreement, much less to administer justice to the combatants.

In the first half of the nineteenth century, the two parties held the nation together because their competition forced them to seek support in both northern and southern states. When slavery became the centerpiece of campaigning, this dynamic led them to tear themselves into sectional pieces. Compromise proposals only exacerbated the coming clash. Congress became the crucible of the combustible mixture rather than a place for deliberation, expostulation, and lawmaking.

From the speeches on both sides during and after the Brooks-Sumner affair, congressmen showed that they reflected their sections culturally and socially rather than a shared, national sentiment. The caning of Charles Sumner appeared in that way in newspapers as well. Secessionists concluded that the two nations should separate as a matter of course.

However, like the economics of slavery and free labor, this too is arguable as a matter of reality, given that, even in revolt, the slaveholding South was divided. Some scholars have argued that the South only became the South as a result of the war. United in the "Lost Cause" defeat, the eleven states of the Confederacy became a distinct region, albeit known for Jim Crow segregation and traditionalism more than anything else.

Finally, the significance of the caning lies in its power as an analogy. Just as Brooks acted against Sumner in 1856, so the Confederates acted against the Union in 1861. Honor and anxiety dictated action, not cool calculation. The parallels are astounding. Although Brooks was no small man at six feet in height, he compared himself unfavorably to Sumner's additional inches and heft. He struck while Sumner was seated. He continued to strike long after his cane had broken and his quarry lay prostrate. The assault projected an anger disproportionate to the offense. Even under the honor code of the South, Brooks behaved untowardly. Something more was involved than avenging language insulting to an elderly relation with the resulting sense of duty.

It is not appropriate to psychoanalyze Brooks or, even worse, his compatriots. We can, however, observe several things about his behavior and that of his fellows that would be manifest in the coming of the war. Brooks and the leaders of the future Confederacy did not act in a political, economic, social, or cultural vacuum. The election cycle, with its effusions of political rhetoric, and the partisan nature of national political parties widened the distance between slavery's advocates and its critics. Sumner's language played into this process, gaining meanings and emphases out of context and giving him a prominence out of proportion to his influence.

One might conclude that the prevalence and persistence of one form of the honor culture in the South and another kind of idealism in the North was the crux of the difference between Sumner and Brooks, North and South, and, ultimately, Union and Confederate. We must remember what Kentucky's Crittenden did in the midst of the fracas. He tried to be neutral, argued for restraint, and attempted to moderate. As such he represented the border states well. Being from a slaveholding state did not mean that one subscribed to an extreme version of the honor culture.

There is more to the story than this clash between cultures, however, because in some respects Brooks was violating the honor culture. By all measures usually employed, he should have challenged Sumner to a duel. We might very well conclude that the honor culture had broken down in this case. The breakdown of civility symbolized in the Brooks-Sumner affair was thus an ominous portent of more than civil disunion. It signaled the end of one kind of nation.

Well into the 1850s, the United States was still a congeries of small towns, counties, and localities. For all the telegraph wires and newspaper plants, it was still a face-to-face society, in which the glue that held society together was common understandings and conventions. These were shared in the North and the South, save for slavery. Indeed, that is what made slavery the peculiar institution.

In the days before the Civil War, the nation changed. It became recognizably modern. In the ever-increasing onslaught of capitalism as culture, commercialism, and the effect of mass media and technologies on the individual identities within those communities, the nation grew not to know itself.

People today are more than familiar with the sense of isolation and commodification in which their lives become just one more statistic in an even larger machine. Once valued in our communities for our contribution as people, Americans now face the reality of interchangeability, cults of celebrity substituting for what was once a celebration of talent or leadership, and the reduction of the ordinary American to a consumer of news, clothing, goods, or services.

Individuals in societies experiencing this transition from the previous traditions to modernity react in many different ways. Sometimes it is a quest for one's own celebrity; sometimes it is an attempt to submerge oneself into a larger cause. The anxiety can lead to darker places such as anger, frustration, and aggression. People in both the North and the South struggled with this transition to modernity. Naturally, many saw a malevolent conspiracy behind it. Humans have seen conspiracies in difficult-to-explain, harmful phenomena for as long as anyone can recall.

Both Brooks and Sumner saw a conspiracy. They just happened to see the conspiracy in the actions of one another. Brooks articulated his view of the abolitionist conspiracy from the North in his speeches and correspondence. Sumner made plain his perception of a slave power conspiracy from the South in his philippics, broadsides, speeches, and letters. That Brooks ultimately reacted to Sumner's attacks on the slave conspiracy was less a divergence of the honor culture from that of the North than the expression of his rage at a personal insult on a public stage.

This is the last measure of the significance of the caning, its almost feral character. Sumner did not provoke the attack. He did not shout epithets directly at Brooks or Butler or South Carolina. In legal terms he did not use "fighting words." The oration's rhetoric was incisive but well within the traditions of classical rhetoric and meant to be. Brooks was well out of the crowded theater, to use Justice Oliver Wendell Holmes Jr.'s metaphor of the clear and present danger of shouting fire in a crowded theater, when he planned and then executed his attack. Brooks reacted in a way that evinces something more visceral than something inspired in the shadow of a contrasting legal system.

To understand how the caning expressed the almost instinctual aggression of the age, one need only return to the metaphors Brooks used in his defense, namely, those of filial duty and what it meant to be a "son." His concepts of manhood, duty, and filial obligation filled his rhetoric and, perhaps more importantly, his psyche. They were not mere flourish. He was not just attempting to appeal to the sympathies or pathos of his audience. He spoke from the heart. While he touched on the romantic themes popular in the literature of the time, this was also the confession of a man not fully in control of his considerable temper.

His rage at Sumner led him to plan not a confrontation but a beating. His actions were those of one seeking to dominate from an inferior position. Brooks was not punishing Sumner as one would punish one's dog. No lover of dogs beat his own. No good parent beat their child into a bloody wreck. One did not even thrash a slave out of anger or into unconsciousness. One administered blows in accordance with right practice. Brooks, on the other hand, unleashed his fury on Sumner in order to lower him as one might fight the bully in the schoolyard—with stealth, swiftness, and completeness.

Brooks's references to the honor culture of the South, his careful planning of the assault, and its ferocious performance reveal him as the epitome of man as territorial being. If Brooks saw himself not above or outside the law, but as the defender of a territory, then he could dispassionately plan and execute what appeared to be a senseless crime. He knew he would be punished for his actions but did them anyway. In his view, they were necessary. His actions mirrored those of the secessionists only a few years later, and they stemmed from the same source. Like him, the secessionists set themselves up as the defenders of a territory, their soil, their land. They would interpret the meaning of the Constitution, not the High Court, the Congress, or the President, to preserve this southern nation against all who threatened it, Sumner included.

Thus, the caning rises above being a mere domino in the events leading up to the Civil War. It tells us a great deal about the cut-and-thrust of politics. It illuminates the transformation of American society, media, and culture into modernity. It reminds us of the basic humanity of those remote political figures whose decisions shaped the course of the nation. It points out the landscape of the law in both the courts and lawmaking bodies. It gives us a revealing look into the concepts of honor that continue to influence us today. It serves as a warning about how our words and deeds can have great consequences. Finally, it places us on notice about the contingencies of history and inevitability in national affairs. We cannot overlook the big and the small when we consider that minute or so on the floor of the Senate chamber on May 22, 1856.

EPILOGUE

WE HAVE traveled a great distance to arrive at this point in our story. From a retelling of that clash on the floor of the U.S. Senate to the states that gave the principal players their backgrounds, from the disputes that culminated in Sumner's "Crime against Kansas" oration to the legal proceedings that followed the caning, from the newspaper coverage to the larger political aftermath, from the disputes after 1856 to the war, which rendered a nation, and finally to the questions of significance, we have looked at objects great and small over the course of the nation's early history. While the story continues into Reconstruction and beyond, we must stop here and ask ourselves one final question: what have we learned?

Without a doubt, the Brooks-Sumner affair still speaks to us. It tells us about the dangers of turning words into violent action. It reminds us that sticks and stones do hurt our bones, and words may lead to sticks and stones. It has become part of the current conversation to lament the decline in civility in American politics. Taking umbrage at political charges is frequently tarnished as just another campaign tactic. "Going negative" in campaign advertising is something regarded as dirty, desperate, and an attempt at distraction from real issues. As such we tend to look at the discourse of the mid-nineteenth century and recoil at its passion, its disparaging attacks, and its length.

Lewis Cass's denunciation of Sumner's "Crime against Kansas" oration is taken at face value. Textbooks decry Sumner's personal references much in the same way Southerners did at the time. Our present-day desire for elevated, neutral, and moderate discourse overrides what may be our sympathy for the objectives Sumner possessed and the fury that Brooks felt.

It is one of the great contradictions in our perceptions of the caning that some modern historians have regarded Sumner as an extremist, the cause of his own travail, and Brooks as justifiably driven to his assault, despite our (almost universal) subscription to Sumner's goals, perspective, and morality and our disavowal of Brooks's. Such misplaced sympathies are the result of a misunderstanding.

We look back on the honor culture from the perspective of a society that still values its tenets of acting according to a code of civility, but not the form it took in mid-nineteenth-century America. Our films, novels, and television shows exhibit a firm grasp of honor's precepts. One can even argue that we have expanded its purview to all of society's members rather than just gentlemen and ladies.

Although we condemn Brooks's assault, we do not condemn the feeling from which it sprung. In this fashion, we can also sympathize with those Confederates who fought the Civil War. They too were defending their homes from invasion, protecting their way of life against encroachment, and sacrificing their lives for a cause. Just as a substantial grave marker denotes the veneration of Brooks, so too do the memorials for the most famous figures of the Confederacy, notably the monumental memorial carved into Stone Mountain in Georgia of Jefferson Davis, Robert E. Lee, and Thomas "Stonewall" Jackson. U.S. Army bases are named after Confederate generals such as A.P. Hill. The "Lost Cause" mythology lives on, although its association with the Ku Klux Klan and other domestic terrorist groups is largely forgotten or concealed. This celebration of the heroism of the Confederate South takes place while simultaneously disavowing the slavery, the violence, and the treason it served.

Thus, the immediate outcome of the caning foretold the reconciliation between the Confederacy and the Union. Just as Brooks received a hero's welcome and a pass from future historians and served no time for his aggravated assault, so too the Confederacy, whose most telling memorial was the death of over three hundred thousand U.S. armed forces personnel, was ultimately rewarded with rehabilitation, forgiveness, and a fine. The losses the war inflicted on the young men of the South and the destruction of homes and families in the conflict were punishment enough. A noted historian has written about this healing process that Lincoln referred to as a mending of the nation's wounds and determined that the reunion was a feature of how humans tend to deal with painful memories.

In such unifying, reconciliation stories, both sides were told that they were wrong and right. The Union and Confederate troops had fought valiantly, courageously, and righteously for their respective causes. The Federals or Yankees, as they are often pejoratively termed in some college textbooks, waged a war for Union and for freedom. The Confederates (rarely called rebels nowadays) fought to defend their homes from invasion. Freeing the slaves and ensuring their rights as citizens, the real and only blessings of the war, are the subjects of an entirely different group of historians and taught, most often, in entirely different courses from the war, as if the two did not belong together.

The ultimate reconciliation of Brooks and Sumner, the Confederacy and the Union in many historical accounts, if not in real life, is not what one should learn from the caning, for it conceals culpability and refuses to inflict pain beyond the wounds that disunion and rebellion actually caused. That too-easy reconciliation would have dire effects on the lives of African-American men and women in the years to come, as Reconstruction, conceived as a great experiment in long-overdue justice, gave way to expediency, forgetting, and continued racial oppression. We must continually examine this history or we will be in jeopardy of learning nothing from it. That would be another tragedy.

ACKNOWLEDGMENTS

THE WRITING of a book incurs many debts. This one is no different. Financial support in the form of a semester-long sabbatical and library services have come from my employer, Seton Hall University. I must also thank my colleagues in the history department, my chair, Maxine Lurie, my dean, Joseph Marbach, and the provost, A. Gabriel Esteban, for approving the sabbatical, without which this project would not have been possible.

Research facilities at the University of Georgia and Rutgers University have also been of material assistance. The South Caroliniana Library at the University of South Carolina gave permission for the use of its holdings, for which I am grateful. I am also grateful for the use of the Seton Hall University Walsh Library and its EZ-Borrow system.

I am also indebted to all the readers of the manuscript for their help in perfecting my prose, arguments, and history. At the press, I owe a debt of thanks to Robert J. Brugger; Jeremy Horsefield, my copy editor; and my anonymous reader. Steve Berry at the University of Georgia helped immensely with several parts of the manuscript. Once again I owe more than I can repay to my mother, N. E. H. Hull, for her unstinting support and willingness to serve as so much more than a sounding board. I owe another unpayable debt to my father, Peter Charles Hoffer, for his editing, advice, ready ear, and ability to deal with his most demanding, obstinate, and challenging student. For all the errors that remain, I take full and complete responsibility.

NOTES

INTRODUCTION

1. Nassim Nicholas Taleb, *The Black Swan: The Impact of the Highly Improbable* (New York: Random House, 2007).

CHAPTER ONE: One Minute

1. Quoted in Orville Vernon Burton, *The Age of Lincoln* (New York: Hill and Wang, 2007), 50.

2. *Congressional Globe*, 36th Cong., 2nd sess., 1305. All references to the *Congressional Globe* are to the version available online through the Library of Congress web site, http://lcweb2.loc.gov/ammem/amlaw/lwcglink.html#anchor35.

3. P. S. Brooks to J. D. Bright, *Congressional Globe*, 36th Cong., 2nd sess., June 2, 1856, 1347.

4. Benjamin Perley Poore, *Perley's Reminiscences of Sixty Years in the National Metropolis*, vol. 1 (New York: AMS Press, 1886), 532–36.

5. Peter Charles Hoffer, *The Treason Trials of Aaron Burr* (Lawrence: University Press of Kansas, 2008), 34.

6. John Lyde Wilson, *The Code of Honor; or Rules for the Government of Principals and Seconds in Duelling* (Charleston, South Carolina: James Phinney, 1858), 10.

7. Samuel Sewall, *The Selling of Joseph* [1700], quoted in "Protests against Slavery in Massachusetts," *Transactions of the Colonial Society of Massachusetts* 8 (1902–4), 287.

8. Cushing, J., charge to the grand jury, *Commonwealth v. Jennison* [1783], unreported, printed in *Proceedings of the Massachusetts Historical Society* (1873–75), 295.

9. Mason Locke Weems, *The Devil in Petticoats, or, God's Revenge against Husband Killing* ([1816] reprinted Edgefield, S.C.: Bacon and Adams, 1878), 3.

CHAPTER TWO: A Machine That Would Go of Itself?

1. Quoted in Don E. Fehrenbacher, *The Dred Scott Case: Its Significance in American Law and Politics* (New York: Oxford University Press, 1978), 105.

2. John C. Calhoun, "The Southern Address," in *The Works and Public Letters of*

John C. Calhoun, vol. 6, ed. Richard K. Crallé (New York: Appleton and Company, 1857), 304.

3. Daniel Webster, "The Constitution and the Union," in *The Great Speeches and Orations of Daniel Webster with an Essay on Daniel Webster as a Master of English Style by Edwin P. Whipple* (Boston: Little, Brown, & Co., 1891), 600.

4. Charles Sumner, "The Landmark of Freedom," in *The Caning of Senator Sumner*, ed. T. Lloyd Benson (Belmont, CA: Thomson-Wadsworth, 2004), 44.

5. Sumner, "Landmark," 46.

6. As quoted in Robert Cover, *Justice Accused: Antislavery and the Judicial Process* (New Haven: Yale University Press, 1975), 156.

7. Andrew P. Butler, "Senator Andrew Butler's Speech on the Nebraska Bill, 24–25 February 1854," in *The Caning*, 52–53.

8. "Nebraska Bill Debates, 3 March 1854," in *The Caning*, 55.

9. *Congressional Globe*, 33rd Cong., 1st sess., 282, as quoted in David Donald, *Charles Sumner and the Coming of the Civil War* (New York: Alfred A. Knopf, 1960), 253.

10. "Sumner's Final Protest against the Nebraska Bill and Remonstrances from the New England Clergy," in *The Caning*, 58.

11. "Senator Mason of Virginia Debates Sumner over Northern Religion and Politics," in *The Caning*, 59.

12. "Sumner's Speech on the Petition to Repeal the Fugitive Slave Act, 26 June 1856," in *The Caning*, 64.

13. "Senator Butler's Reply to Sumner," in *The Caning*, 66.

14. "Senator Mason's Reply to Sumner," in *The Caning*, 67, 68.

15. "Senator Clay Attacks Sumner," in *The Caning*, 68, 69.

16. "Sumner's Reply to Assailants and Oath to Support the Constitution," in *The Caning*, 70–73.

17. "Sumner's Reply," in *The Caning*, 70.

18. "Senator Butler's Final Response," in *The Caning*, 77, 84.

19. Charles Sumner, *The Crime against Kansas* (New York: Arno Press & The New York Times, 1969), 9.

20. Sumner, *The Crime*, 5.

21. Sumner, *The Crime*, 32.

22. Sumner, *The Crime*, 43.

23. Sumner, *The Crime*, 61.

24. Sumner, *The Crime*, 85, 87.

25. Sumner, *The Crime*, 94.

26. Henry Wilson, *The History of the Rise and Fall of the Slave Power in America*, vol. 2 (Boston: J. R. Osgood and Company, 1874), 479.

27. *Congressional Globe*, 34th Cong., 1st sess., Appendix, 545, 544.

28. P. S. Brooks to Hon. J. D. Bright, President of the Senate, *Congressional Globe*, 34th Cong., 1st sess., 1347.

CHAPTER THREE: Immediate Aftermath

1. *Congressional Globe*, 33rd Cong., 1st sess., March 15, 1854, Appendix, 371, 372.

2. *Congressional Globe*, 33rd Cong., 1st sess., June 14, 1854, Appendix, 924, 926.

3. *Congressional Globe*, 33rd Cong., 1st sess., June 21, 1854, 1466, 1477.

4. *Congressional Globe*, 34th Cong., 1st sess., December 24, 1855, 77.

5. *Congressional Globe*, 34th Cong., 1st sess., January 9, 1856, 189.

6. *Congressional Globe*, 34th Cong., 1st sess., July 14, 1856, Appendix, 832.

7. David Donald, *Charles Sumner and the Coming of the Civil War* (New York: Alfred A. Knopf, 1960), 289.

8. *Congressional Globe*, 34th Cong., 1st sess., June 13, 1856, Appendix, 632.

9. *Congressional Globe*, 34th Cong., 1st sess., December 24, 1856, 77.

10. *Congressional Globe*, 34th Cong., 1st sess., June 2, 1856, 1366.

11. *Congressional Globe*, 34th Cong., 1st sess., May 27, 1856, 1306, 1305.

12. Henry Wilson, *History of the Rise and Fall of the Slave Power in America*, vol. 2 (Boston: James R. Osgood and Company, 1874), 487.

13. *Congressional Globe*, 34th Cong., 1st sess., June 2, 1856, 1349.

14. *Congressional Globe*, 34th Cong., 1st sess., June 2, 1856, 1353; May 27, 1856, 1305.

15. "Brooks' Defense of Himself," *New York Times*, July 10, 1856; *Congressional Globe*, 34th Cong., 1st sess., June 2, 1856, 1360.

16. *Congressional Globe*, 34th Cong., 1st sess., June 2, 1856, 1360.

17. *Congressional Globe*, 34th Cong., 1st sess., June 11, 1856, 1361.

18. *Congressional Globe*, 34th Cong., 1st sess., June 2, 1856, 1364.

19. *Congressional Globe*, 34th Cong., 1st sess., July 14, 1856, 1014.

20. *Congressional Globe*, 34th Cong., 1st sess., July 14, 1856, Appendix, 831.

21. *Congressional Globe*, 34th Cong., 1st sess., July 16, 1856, Appendix, 833, 837.

22. Charles Sumner, *The Works of Charles Sumner*, vol. 4 (Boston: Lee and Shepard, 1875), 269–70.

23. "Brooks' Defense of Himself, from the Washington Union," *New York Times*, July 10, 1856.

24. Ibid.

25. Preston S. Brooks, Private Correspondence, in "Preston S. Brooks on the Caning of Charles Sumner," ed. Robert L. Meriwether, *The South Carolina Historical and Genealogical Magazine* 52 (4) (Oct. 1951): 3–4, 2–3.

26. Brooks, "The Caning," 2, 3.

27. "Statement by Preston S. Brooks," *Proceedings of the Massachusetts Historical Society* 61 (1928): 221–23; "Statement of Mr. Brooks," Preston S. Brooks Papers, No. 7951, Folder 3, South Caroliniana Library.

28. Brayton Harris, *Blue & Gray in Black & White: Newspapers in the Civil War* (Washington, DC: Brassey's, 2000), 15.

29. For a collection of editorials on the caning see Benson, *The Caning*, and his Web site, "Secession Era Editorials Project," History Department, Furman Univer-

sity, http://history.furman.edu/editorials/see.py?menu=sumenu&sequence=sumen u&location=%3E%20Sumner%20Caning%20.

30. Avery Craven, *The Coming of the Civil War*, 2nd ed. (Chicago: University of Chicago Press, 1942, 1969), 374–77; *The Growth of Southern Nationalism, 1848–1861; A History of the South*, vol. 6, ed. Wendell Holmes Stephenson and E. Merton Coulter (Baton Rouge: Louisiana State University Press, 1953), 229–36; David Donald, *Charles Sumner and the Coming of the Civil War* (New York: Alfred A. Knopf, 1960), 304–10.

31. David Tatham, "Pictorial Responses to the Caning of Senator Sumner," in *American Printmaking before 1876: Fact, Fiction, and Fantasy, Papers Presented at a Symposium Held at the Library of Congress, June 12 and 13, 1972* (Washington, DC: Library of Congress, 1975), 11–19.

32. Brooks, "The Caning," 4.

33. As quoted in Robert Neil Mathis, "Preston Smith Brooks: The Man and His Image," *South Carolina Historical Magazine* 79 (Oct. 1978): 307.

CHAPTER FOUR: A Long, Winding Road

1. W. A. Swanberg, *Sickles the Incredible* (Gettysburg: Stan Clark Military Books, 1984), 19.

2. "Abraham Lincoln's 'House Divided' Speech, June 16, 1858," in Michael F. Holt, *The Fate of Their Country: Politicians, Slavery Extension, and the Coming of the Civil War* (New York: Hill and Wang, 2004), 146.

3. William H. Seward, *The Works of William H. Seward*, vol. 4, ed. George E. Baker (Boston: Houghton Mifflin and Company, 1884), 292, 298.

4. David S. Reynolds, *John Brown, Abolitionist* (New York: Alfred A. Knopf, 2005), 159.

5. Henry David Thoreau, *A Plea for Captain John Brown* [Read to the Citizens of Concord, Mass., on October 30, 1859] (Whitefish, MT: Kessinger Publishing, 2004).

6. *Congressional Globe*, 36th Cong., 1st sess., Appendix, 88–93, as quoted in David M. Potter, *The Impending Crisis, 1848–1861*, ed. Don E. Fehrenbacher (New York: Harper & Row, 1976), 383.

7. James Ford Rhodes, *History of the United States from the Compromise of 1850*, vol. 2 (New York: Harper and Brothers Publishers, 1893), 420.

8. Potter, *Impending Crisis*, 389.

9. Abraham Lincoln, *The Collected Works of Abraham Lincoln*, vol. 3, ed. Roy P. Basler (New Brunswick, NJ: Rutgers University Press, 1953), 550.

10. Civil Rights Act of 1875, 18 Stat. Part III, 335 (Act of Mar. 1, 1875), chap. 114.

11. 109 U.S. 3 (1883).

12. *Heart of Atlanta Motel v. United States*, 379 U.S. 241 (1964).

ESSAY ON SOURCES

The notes to this book are reserved for direct quotations from primary sources. My debt to the many fine works on the caning and the politics of the 1850s and all the other topics involved should be obvious from the essay below. What follows is a necessarily brief overview of the works that became a part of the preceding narrative on the caning and its origins, impact, and emblematic or representational value.

There are several articles and unpublished dissertations that cover the caning, including William E. Gienapp, "The Crime against Sumner: The Caning of Charles Sumner and the Rise of the Republican Party," *Civil War History*, 25 (3) (1979): 218–45; Manisha Sinha, "The Caning of Charles Sumner: Slavery, Race, and Ideology in the Age of the Civil War," *Journal of the Early Republic*, 23 (summer 2003): 233–62; Sylvia D. Hoffert, "The Brooks-Sumner Affair: Prelude to Civil War," *Civil War Times Illustrated*, 11 (Oct. 1972): 35–40; Laura A. White, "Was Charles Sumner Shamming, 1856–1859?" *The New England Quarterly*, 33 (3) (Sept. 1960): 291–324; Harlan Joel Gradin, "Losing Control: The Caning of Charles Sumner and the Breakdown of Antebellum Political Culture," PhD diss., University of North Carolina at Chapel Hill, 1991; Kenneth A. Deitreich, "Honor, Patriarchy, and Disunion: Masculinity and the Coming of the American Civil War," PhD diss., West Virginia University, 2006; and Catherine Clinton, "Sex and the Sectional Conflict," *Taking Off the White Gloves: Southern Women and Women Historians*, edited by Michele Gillespie and Catherine Clinton (Columbia, MO: University of Missouri Press, 1998).

There are a great many books on the era of the caning, frequently referred to as the crisis of the 1850s. This work has made use of many of them, but by far not all. More complete lists of books and articles on the origins of the Civil War may be found in Kenneth M. Stampp, *The Causes of the Civil War*, Revised Edition (New York: Touchstone, 1991); and the "Suggestions for Further Reading" in Michael Holt's brief and readable *The Fate of Their Country: Politicians, Slavery Extension, and the Coming of the Civil War* (New York: Hill and Wang, 2004). For the seminal books on the 1850s, I used Avery Craven, *The Coming of the Civil War* (Chicago: University of Chicago Press, 1957); David M. Potter, *The Impending Crisis, 1848–1861*, completed and edited by Don E. Fehrenbacher (New York: Harper and Row, 1976); William W. Freehling, *The Road to Disunion, Volume 1, Secessionists at Bay, 1776–1854* (New York: Oxford University Press, 1990), *The Road to Disunion, Volume 2, Secessionists Triumphant, 1854–1861* (New York: Oxford University Press, 2007); Michael F. Holt, *The Political Crisis of the 1850s* (New York: John Wiley, 1978); Bruce Levine, *Half Slave and Half*

Free: The Roots of the Civil War (New York: Hill and Wang, 1992); the multiple essays in *Why the Civil War Came*, edited by Gabor S. Boritt (New York: Oxford University Press, 1996); Edward L. Ayers, *What Caused the Civil War? Reflections on the South and Southern History* (New York: W. W. Norton, 2005); and Kenneth M. Stampp, *The Imperiled Union: Essays on the Background of the Civil War* (New York: Oxford University Press, 1980); Mark W. Summers, *The Plundering Generation: Corruption and the Crisis of the Union, 1849–1861* (New York: Oxford University Press, 1987); and Jean Harvey Baker, "Politics, Paradigms, and Public Culture," *The Journal of American History*, 84 (3) (Dec. 1997): 894–99.

Violence in the U.S. Congress has its own chroniclers. I used Joanne B. Freeman, *Affairs of Honor: National Politics in the New Republic* (New Haven: Yale University Press, 2001); *Deseret News* (Salt Lake City), "Notable Incivilities Past," in 2004, available from the Internet; Alvin M. Josephy Jr., *On the Hill: A History of the American Congress, from 1789 to the Present* (New York: Simon and Schuster, 1979); Joseph West Moore, *The American Congress: A History of National Legislation and Political Events, 1774–1895* (New York: Harper & Brothers Publishers, 1895); Robert V. Remini, *The House: The History of the House of Representatives* (New York: HarperCollins, 2006); and Shelley Ross, *Fall from Grace: Sex, Scandal, and Corruption in American Politics from 1702 to the Present* (New York: Ballantine Books, 1988).

For the individual incidents, topical accounts are the place to look. The Sam Houston–William Stanbery exchange is retold in Herman J. Viola, "Indian Rations and Sam Houston's Trial," in *Congress Investigates, 1792–1974*, edited by Arthur M. Schlesinger and Roger Bruns (New York: Chelsea House Publishers, 1975). The Lyon-Griswold fracas is covered in Brian T. Neff, "Fracas in Congress: The Battle of Honor between Matthew Lyon and Roger Griswold," *Essays in History*, 41 (1999), http://etext.virginia.edu/journals/EH/EH41/Neff41.html, among others. The Rust-Greeley confrontation is part of every biography of Horace Greeley, a major figure in mid-nineteenth-century politics, including Jeter Allen Isley, *Horace Greeley and the Republican Party, 1853–1861: A Study of the New York Tribune* (Princeton: Princeton University Press, 1947); and Glyndon G. Van Deusen, *Horace Greeley: Nineteenth Century Crusader* (New York: Hill and Wang, 1953).

The honor culture has a copious literature with an emphasis on developments in the South rather than the North. For the preceding I consulted Edward Pessen, "How Different from Each Other Were the Antebellum North and South," *The American Historical Review*, 85 (5) (Dec. 1980): 1119–49; Michael Stephen Hindus, *Prison and Plantation: Crime, Justice, and Authority in Massachusetts and South Carolina, 1767–1878* (Chapel Hill: University of North Carolina Press, 1980); Bertram Wyatt-Brown, *Yankee Saints and Southern Sinners* (Baton Rouge: Louisiana State University Press, 1985); *Honor and Violence in the Old South* (New York: Oxford University Press, 1986); *The Shaping of Southern Culture: Honor, Grace, and War, 1760s–1880s* (Chapel Hill: University of North Carolina Press, 2001); *Southern Honor: Ethics and Behavior in the Old South* (New York: Oxford University Press, 2007); Edward L. Ayers, *Vengeance and Justice: Crime and Punishment in the Nineteenth-Century American South* (New

York: Oxford University Press, 1984); Kenneth Greenberg, *Honor & Slavery* (Princeton: Princeton University Press, 1996); *Masters and Statesmen: The Political Culture of American Slavery* (Baltimore: Johns Hopkins University Press, 1988); Dickson D. Bruce Jr., *Violence and Culture in the Antebellum South* (Austin: University of Texas Press, 1979); and Elliott J. Gorn's colorful "'Gouge and Bite, Pull Hair and Scratch': The Social Significance of Fighting in the Southern Backcountry," *American Historical Review*, 90 (1) (Feb. 1985): 18–43.

For South Carolina's general problems with crime, with attention to Edgefield, consult Jack Kenny Williams, *Vogues in Villainy: Crime and Retribution in Ante-bellum South Carolina* (Columbia: University of South Carolina Press, 1959); and his *Dueling in the Old South: Vignettes of Social History* (College Station: Texas A&M University Press, 1980), for an exposition on the topic as well as a reprint of John Lyde Wilson's *The Code of Honor*. Edgefield has its own chronicler in Orville Vernon Burton, *In My Father's House Are Many Mansions: Family and Community in Edgefield, South Carolina* (Chapel Hill: University of North Carolina Press, 1985).

The economic and social context that gave rise to the politics of the 1850s is dealt with in several volumes, including Jonathan H. Earle, *Jacksonian Antislavery & the Politics of Free Soil, 1824–1854* (Chapel Hill: University of North Carolina Press, 2004); David A. Hounshell, *From the American System to Mass Production, 1800–1932* (Baltimore: Johns Hopkins University Press, 1984); Daniel Walker Howe, *The Political Culture of the American Whigs* (Chicago: University of Chicago Press, 1984); Richard L. McCormick, *The Party Period and Public Policy: American Politics from the Age of Jackson to the Progressive Era* (New York: Oxford University Press, 1989); Alexander Saxton, *The Rise and Fall of the White Republic: Class Politics and Mass Culture in Nineteenth Century America* (New York: Verso, 1990); Charles Sellers, *The Market Revolution: Jacksonian America, 1815–1846* (New York: Oxford University Press, 1991); George Rogers Taylor, *The Transportation Revolution, 1815–1860* (Armonk, NY: M. E. Sharpe, 1951, 1989); and Harry L. Watson, *Liberty and Power: The Politics of Jacksonian America* (New York: Noonday Press, 1990).

There are a great many books and articles on the North, Massachusetts, and Charles Sumner. A good, recent, short biography of Sumner is Frederick J. Blue, *Charles Sumner and the Conscience of the North* (Arlington Heights, IL: Harlan Davidson, 1994). David H. Donald's prize-winning biography, *Charles Sumner and the Coming of the Civil War* (New York: Alfred A. Knopf, 1960), is required reading despite errors and the misleading use of evidence to create a largely negative portrait. For a critique of Donald see Anne-Marie Taylor, *Young Charles Sumner and the Legacy of the American Enlightenment, 1811–1851* (Amherst: University of Massachusetts Press, 2001). On abolitionism, I drew from Paul Goodman, *Of One Blood: Abolitionism and the Origins of Racial Equality* (Berkeley: University of California Press, 2000); Stanley Harrold, *American Abolitionists* (Harlow, England: Pearson Education Limited, 2001); and Ronald G. Walters, *The Antislavery Appeal: American Abolitionism after 1830* (Baltimore: Johns Hopkins University Press, 1976). Two excellent volumes on the legal arguments of the American antislavery movement are Robert Cover, *Justice Accused:*

Antislavery and the Judicial Process (New Haven: Yale University Press, 1975); and William M. Wiecek, *The Sources of Antislavery Constitutionalism in America, 1760–1848* (Ithaca: Cornell University Press, 1977).

There are several books, articles, and dissertations written on Brooks, slavery, and the South. They include John Hope Franklin, *The Militant South, 1800–1861* (Urbana: University of Illinois Press, 1956, 2002); Avery O. Craven, *The Growth of Southern Nationalism, 1848–1861, A History of the South, Volume VI*, edited by Wendell Holmes Stephenson and E. Merton Coulter (Baton Rouge: Louisiana State University Press, 1953); James C. Cobb, *Away Down South: A History of Southern Identity* (New York: Oxford University, 2005); Stanley M. Elkins, *Slavery: A Problem in American Institutional and Intellectual Life*, Third Edition, Revised (Chicago: University of Chicago Press, 1976); Robert William Fogel and Stanley L. Engerman, *Time on the Cross: The Economics of American Negro Slavery* (Boston: Little Brown, 1974), 2 vols.; Sally E. Hadden, *Slave Patrols: Law and Violence in Virginia and the Carolinas* (Cambridge: Harvard University Press, 2001); Christine Leigh Heyrman, *Southern Cross: The Beginnings of the Bible Belt* (Chapel Hill: University of North Carolina Press, 1997); Thomas D. Morris, *Southern Slavery and the Law, 1619–1860* (Chapel Hill: University of North Carolina Press, 1996); and Kenneth M. Stampp, *The Peculiar Institution: Slavery in the Ante-Bellum South* (New York: Alfred A. Knopf, 1956).

For South Carolina in particular, one should read Walter Edgar, *South Carolina: A History* (Columbia: University of South Carolina Press, 1998); Lacy K. Ford, *Origins of Southern Radicalism: The South Carolina Upcountry, 1800–1860* (New York: Oxford University Press, 1988); Rachel N. Klein, *Unification of a Slave State: The Rise of the Planter Class in the South Carolina Backcountry, 1760–1808* (Chapel Hill: University of North Carolina Press, 1990); Harold S. Schultz, *Nationalism and Sectionalism in South Carolina, 1852–1860* (New York: Da Capo Press, 1969); and Manisha Sinha, *The Counterrevolution of Slavery* (Chapel Hill: University of North Carolina Press, 2000).

In addition to the sources listed above, there are several works on Preston S. Brooks, Laurence M. Keitt, and Louis T. Wigfall. One should examine Robert Neil Mathis, "Preston Smith Brooks: The Man and His Image," *South Carolina Historical and Genealogical Magazine*, 79 (1978): 296–311; Stephen W. Berry II, *All That Makes a Man* (New York: Oxford University Press, 2002); J. Holt Merchant, "Laurence M. Keitt: South Carolina Fire-Eater," PhD diss., University of Virginia, 1976; Eric Harry Walther, "The Fire-Eaters, the South, and Secession (Volumes I and II)," PhD diss., Louisiana State University, 1988; Alvy L. King, *Louis T. Wigfall: Southern Fire-eater* (Baton Rouge: Louisiana State University Press, 1970); and C. W. Lord, "Young Louis Wigfall: South Carolina Politician and Duelist," *South Carolina Historical and Genealogical Magazine*, 59 (1958): 96–112.

Stephen A. Douglas's life and involvement in these events are still controversial. Biographies include William Gardner, *The Life of Stephen A. Douglas* (Boston: Roxburgh Press, 1905); James L. Huston, *Stephen A. Douglas and the Dilemmas of Democratic Equality* (Lanham, MD: Rowman & Littlefield Publishers, 2007); Robert W. Johannsen, *Stephen A. Douglas* (Urbana: University of Illinois Press, 1997); and Allen Johnson, *Stephen A. Douglas: A Study in American Politics* (New York: Da Capo Press, 1970). The books on the Lincoln-Douglas debates include Frank L. Dennis, *The Lincoln-Douglas Debates* (New York: Mason & Lipscomb Publishers, 1974); Timothy S. Good, *The Lincoln-Douglas Debates and the Making of a President* (Jefferson, NC: McFarland & Company, 2007); and Henry V. Jaffa, *Crisis of the House Divided: An Interpretation of the Issues in the Lincoln-Douglas Debates* (Chicago: University of Chicago Press, 2009).

There are several works that hone in on aspects of the politics of the 1850s. I began with Eric Foner, *Free Soil, Free Labor, Free Men: The Ideology of the Republican Party before the Civil War* (New York: Oxford University Press, 1995); and continued with William E. Gienapp, *The Origins of the Republican Party, 1852–1856* (New York: Oxford University Press, 1987); George H. Mayer, *The Republican Party, 1854–1964* (New York: Oxford University Press, 1964); Malcolm Moos, *The Republicans: A History of Their Party* (New York: Random House, 1956); Joel H. Silbey, "After the 'First Northern Victory': The Republican Party Comes to Congress, 1855–1856," *Journal of Interdisciplinary History*, 20 (1) (summer 1989): 1–24; Leonard L. Richards, *The Slave Power: The Free North and Southern Domination, 1780–1860* (Baton Rouge: Louisiana State University Press, 2000); and Dale Baum, "Know-Nothingism and the Republican Majority in Massachusetts: The Political Realignment of the 1850s," *Journal of American History*, 64 (4) (Mar. 1978): 959–86.

The events in Kansas have spawned their own literature. These works include Nicole Etcheson, *Bleeding Kansas: Contested Liberty in the Civil War Era* (Lawrence: University Press of Kansas, 2004); Victoria Lea Fossett, "May 1856: Southern Reaction to Conflict in Kansas and Congress," MS thesis, University of North Texas, 2007; Craig Miner, *Seeding Civil War: Kansas in the National News, 1854–1858* (Lawrence: University Press of Kansas, 2008); and Gerald W. Wolff, *The Kansas-Nebraska Bill: Party, Section, and the Coming of the Civil War* (New York: Revisionist Press, 1977).

There are several pieces that analyze Sumner's "Crime against Kansas" speech besides those by his many biographers and those writing on the crisis of the 1850s, including Michael D. Pierson, "'All Southern Society Is Assailed by the Foulest Charges': Charles Sumner's 'The Crime against Kansas' and the Escalation of Republican Anti-Slavery Rhetoric," *New England Quarterly*, 68 (4) (Dec. 1995): 531–57; Michael William Pfau, "Time, Tropes, and Textuality: Reading Republicanism in Charles Sumner's 'Crime against Kansas,'" *Rhetoric & Public Affairs*, 6 (3) (2003): 385–414; *The Political Style of Conspiracy: Chase, Sumner, and Lincoln* (East Lansing: Michigan State University Press, 2005); and Andrew W. Robertson, *The Language of Democracy: Political Rhetoric in the United States and Britain, 1790–1900* (Charlottesville: University of Virginia Press, 2005). For the law of libel as it was understood in antebellum America, see Norman L. Rosenberg, *Protecting the Best Men: An Interpretive History of the Law of Libel* (Chapel Hill: University of North Carolina Press, 1986).

Information on both Francis Barton Key, the prosecutor in the Brooks trial, and Thomas H. Crawford, the judge in the trial, is available from Nat Brandt, *The Con-*

gressman Who Got Away with Murder (Syracuse: Syracuse University Press, 1991); Thomas Keneally, *American Scoundrel: The Life of the Notorious Civil War General Dan Sickles* (New York: Anchor Books, 2002); W. A. Swanberg, *Sickles the Incredible* (Gettysburg, PA: Stan Clark Military Books, 2004); and Josephine Pacheco, *The Pearl: A Failed Slave Escape on the Potomac* (Chapel Hill: University of North Carolina Press, 2005).

Scholarship about newspapers in the mid-nineteenth century is very extensive. Background can be found in Brayton Harris, *Blue & Gray in Black & White: Newspapers in the Civil War* (Washington, DC: Brassey's, 2000); Hazel Dicken-Garcia, *Journalistic Standards in Nineteenth-Century America* (Madison: University of Wisconsin Press, 1989); William Huntzicker, *The Popular Press, 1833–1865* (Westport, CT: Greenwood Press, 1999); Trish Loughran, *The Republic in Print: Print Culture in the Age of U.S. Nation Building, 1770–1870* (New York: Columbia University Press, 2007); and Lorman A. Ratner and Dwight L. Teeter Jr., *Fanatics & Fire-Eaters: Newspapers and the Coming of the Civil War* (Urbana: University of Illinois Press, 2003).

For the years following the assault, I used James L. Huston, *The Panic of 1857 and the Coming of the Civil War* (Baton Rouge: Louisiana State University Press, 1987); Kenneth M. Stampp, *America in 1857: A Nation on the Brink* (New York: Oxford University Press, 1990); and Elbert B. Smith, *The Presidency of James Buchanan* (Lawrence: University Press of Kansas, 1975). For the *Dred Scott* case see the very substantial Don E. Fehrenbacher, *The Dred Scott Case: Its Significance in American Law and Politics* (New York: Oxford University Press, 1978); *Slavery, Law, & Politics: The Dred Scott Case in Historical Perspective* (New York: Oxford University Press, 1981); Walker Lewis, *Without Fear or Favor: A Biography of Chief Justice Roger Brooke Taney* (Boston: Houghton Mifflin Company, 1965); and Carl Brent Swisher, *Roger B. Taney* (Hamden, CT: Archon Books, 1961).

Hinton Rowan Helper has received two scholarly treatments. There is J. J. Cardoso, "Hinton Rowan Helper as a Racist in the Abolitionist Camp," *Journal of Negro History*, 55 (4) (Oct. 1970): 323–30; and Joseph Gustaitis, "Southern-born Hinton Helper—Not Harriet Beecher Stowe—Wrote the Most Stinging Indictment of Slavery," *America's Civil War*, 10 (6) (Jan 1998): 8–10.

The architect and symbol of Harpers Ferry receives biographical treatments in Stephen B. Oates, *To Purge This Land with Blood: A Biography of John Brown* (New York: Harper Torchbooks, 1970); and David S. Reynolds, *John Brown, Abolitionist* (New York: Alfred A. Knopf, 2005). The raid itself is the focus of *His Soul Goes Marching On: Responses to John Brown and the Harpers Ferry Raid*, edited by Paul Finkelman (Charlottesville: University Press of Virginia, 1995); and Allan Keller, *Thunder at Harper's Ferry* (Englewood Cliffs: Prentice-Hall, 1958).

The Civil War is covered in several noteworthy volumes. They include William W. Freehling, *The South vs. The South: How Anti-Confederate Southerners Shaped the Course of the Civil War* (New York: Oxford University Press, 2001); James M. McPherson, *Battle Cry of Freedom: The Civil War Era* (New York: Oxford University Press, 1988); Allan Nevins, *The War for the Union* (New York: Collier Books, 1959–1971), 4 vols.;

and Richard Franklin Bensel, *Yankee Leviathan: The Origins of Central State Authority in America, 1859–1877* (Cambridge: Cambridge University Press, 1990).

The long-term impact of the war can be seen in several different areas, including Theda Skocpol, *Protecting Soldiers and Mothers: The Political Origins of Social Policy in the United States* (Cambridge: Belknap Press of Harvard University Press, 1992); Eric Foner, *Reconstruction: America's Unfinished Revolution, 1863–1877* (New York: Perennial Classics, 2002); Michael Les Benedict, *The Blessings of Liberty: A Concise History of the Constitution of the United States*, Second Edition (Boston: Houghton Mifflin, 2006); Peter Charles Hoffer, Williamjames Hull Hoffer, and N. E. H. Hull, *The Supreme Court: An Essential History* (Lawrence: University Press of Kansas, 2007); Thomas Adams Upchurch, *Legislating Racism: The Billion Dollar Congress and the Birth of Jim Crow* (Lexington: University Press of Kentucky, 2004); and Michael Vorenberg, *Final Freedom: The Civil War, the Abolition of Slavery, and the Thirteenth Amendment* (Cambridge: Cambridge University Press, 2001).

The counterfactual is a frequently used device. Daniel Boorstin, *Cleopatra's Nose: Essays on the Unexpected in History* (New York: Random House, 1994); and Peter Charles Hoffer, *The Historians' Paradox* (New York: New York University Press, 2008), both deal with the importance of and problems with this tool. Robert Cowley has edited a series of books on various counterfactual scenarios, including *What Ifs? of American History* (New York: Berkley Books, 2003).

INDEX

Page numbers in italics indicate illustrations.